FREELANCE
DESIGN **IN PRACTICE**

For more excellent books and resources for designers,
visit www.howdesign.com.

13 12 11 10 09   5 4 3 2 1

Distributed in Canada by Fraser Direct
100 Armstrong Avenue
Georgetown, Ontario, Canada L7G 5S4
Tel: (905) 877-4411

Library of Congress Cataloging-in-Publication Data

ISBN: 978-1-60061-302-9

Designed by Hoop Design
Art directed by Tony Seddon

FREELANCE
DESIGN **IN PRACTICE**

DON'T START WORK WITHOUT IT

CATHY FISHEL

HOW
BOOKS

Cincinnati, Ohio
www.howdesign.com

Contents

❶ An illustration of Portobello Market for Soho House's *House* magazine by Adam Hayes, a freelance designer and illustrator working in London, UK.

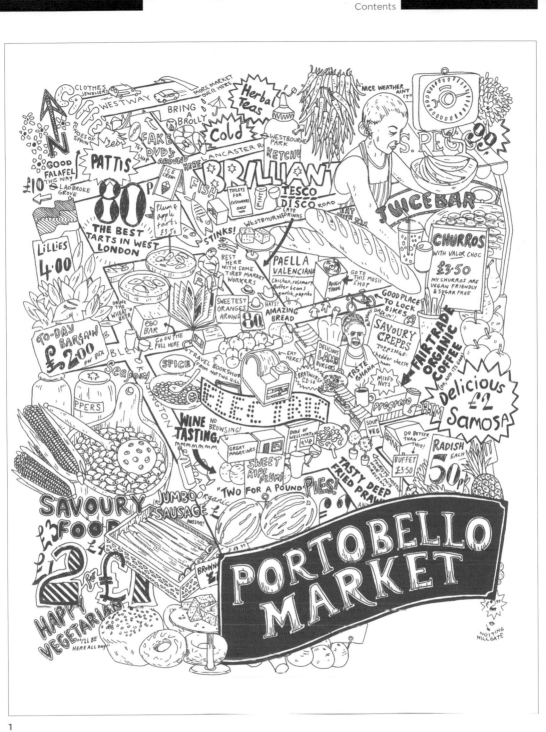

Introduction

"Freelance" is a word inspired by medieval mercenaries who, with allegiance to no liege, made themselves available to those who were willing to pay for their "free" or available lances.

Have things changed all that much? Despite the pejorative term "mercenary," isn't the freelancer a noble soldier who lives on his own terms, always scanning the horizon for opportunity and making his talents available when and where he wishes? Isn't it still a life of freedom and adventure?

On the surface, it does seem romantic—heroic, even. But when you start to think about paying hefty self-employment taxes and health insurance premiums; the endless stream of agonizing but necessary cold calls; clients who refuse to call back, and/or be happy, and/or pay; inadequate or unaffordable office space; the website that needs to be designed, walked, and fed regularly; balancing workflow and cash flow; that gelatinous, yet-to-be determined pricing system... well, pretty soon your steed is galloping off into the sunset alone, leaving you with your puny lance/mouse/pencil and a terrible sense of misgiving. The "free" in "freelance" starts to lose its luster.

"People often tell me that it must be great to choose my own hours, and I respond by saying, 'Yes, all 24 of them,'" quips Rodney Davidson, a long-time freelancer from Alabama, US, and contributor to this book.

Anatomy of a successful freelance designer
Here's what you absolutely, positively have to have to make it:

- You must be confident in the power of your work and skills.

- You must know the best time to start your new venture and be properly prepared for that moment.

- You must be able to withstand risk and its good buddy, stress.

- You must be an extrovert (or possess the ability to do a darn good imitation of one).

- You must value other people and their opinions.

- You must be extremely well organized.

- You must truly want to help others.

- You must be an excellent communicator through design as well as the spoken and written word.

- You must be able to withstand relentless rejection, yet be capable of maintaining boundaries.

- You must be an efficient businessperson and possess a vision for yourself that will drive every business plan and decision that follows.

- You must be objective about your strengths and weaknesses, and address them accordingly.

- You must be able to balance work and life so that you remain happy and healthy.

Let's cut through the rosy haze: a freelance designer is a smart businessperson and talented artist—not a knight, not a renegade, not a *bon vivant* who can work in his or her pajamas all day—who provides design services to people who will pay for them. Sure, you may be a fantastic designer, and you may have your freedom, but there's a lot more to it than that.

It's like a freelance friend told me when I set out many years ago to become a freelance writer: "It's the most terrifying fun you'll ever have."

His words have proved to be true nearly every single day. And for those who choose to make freelancing a career, not a default position to fill in between jobs, there's another quote you'll hear again and again, spoken straight from the heart:

"I could never go back to working for someone else."

It's so true.

This book will help you maintain your independence by giving you real-life, heartfelt advice from people who have made it in the freelance world. Their shared experiences will help you make the wisest decisions in a career that is truly like no other.

So You Want to be a Freelance Designer?

What Makes a Successful Freelancer?

Mia had woken up this morning with a pounding heart. The clock read 7 a.m. and her train would be leaving in exactly half an hour. It was a few seconds before she remembered that there would be no rushing off to the station today. She had resigned from a lucrative but creatively unsatisfying position with a downtown advertising agency, and today, she began her new life as a freelance graphic designer. Her small but cozy studio was all set up and waiting for her downstairs.

After rewarding herself with a few more luxurious minutes wrapped in the bedsheets, her heart began to wobble again. Had she saved enough money to get the business started? Would her former employers really give her work as they had promised? Did she need an accountant or could she handle the billing? How would she get her website up this week, and finish her stationery system? And then there were the cold calls... uncomfortable, awkward intrusions into the lives of preoccupied businesspeople who probably wouldn't hire her anyway.

Suddenly, the train and its destination seemed a lot more comfortable.

Do you have what it takes?

That's not a challenge, it's an honest question. A brand-new freelance designer can have the best planning and resources in place, but without confidence, the whole process grinds to a halt. But confidence alone is not enough. Neither is a bulging contacts book, an efficient office space, or even unbeatable talent, schooling, or previous experience.

For the individual who wants to make a success of being a freelance designer, all of the pieces have to be in place. But there's one other component, a magic word that binds everything together, a mantra that will get you through the toughest days. It's a word that might be worth pasting over your computer: *yagaddawanna*.

In more conventional parlance, *you have got to want it*—really want it. There are thousands of designers who resort to freelancing as a default or stopgap between jobs. There are those who freelance on the side for extra cash or more/different/better creative opportunities. But those who truly want to make it as a full-time, long-term, successful freelance designer *have got to want it.* There's absolutely no one else out there that can make it happen but you.

"If you fail as a freelancer, It's something that *you* caused. There is a direct correlation between your efforts and your success."

Angela Ferraro-Fanning, 13thirty-one Design, Wisconsin, US

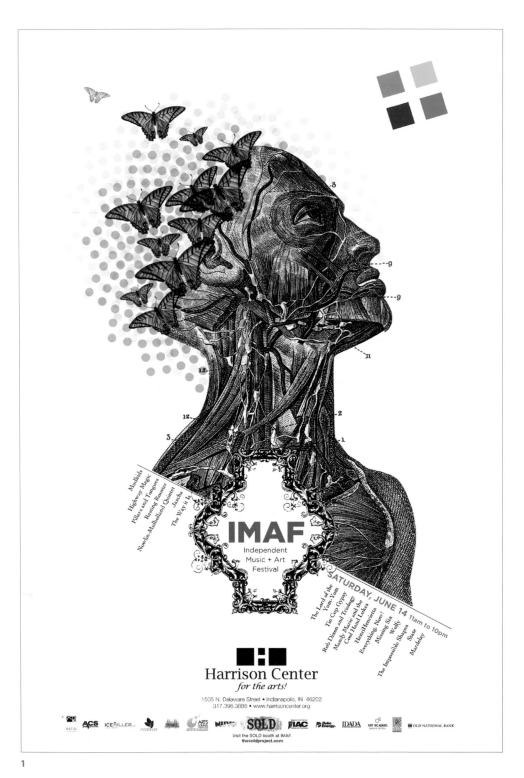

What skills must you have?

The following attributes and skills, listed in no particular order, were cited by freelance designers from all over the world. Consider these alongside the list in the Introduction (see pages 8–9), and decide whether you've got what it takes to make it as a freelance designer.

- Confidence in what you do.

- Passion for what you do.

- An open mind that can consider the ideas of others.

- A can-do attitude when it comes to solving tough design problems and working within various client cultures.

- Honesty with yourself about the skills and talents you have or need to acquire.

- Contentment with your own company, combined with the desire to stay in touch with the outside world.

- The ability to encourage yourself when needed.

- The ability to block out distraction, to concentrate, and take a task to its very end.

- The ability to listen.

- The ability to ask questions.

- The ability to communicate, not just design.

- The ability to accept criticism.

- Be self-motivated, intuitive, and outgoing—a self-starter.

- Good marketing skills: be able to sell yourself and explain what you do.

- Good business skills.

- Good writing skills.

- Good production skills.

- Good computer/technical skills.

1 For her design work for The Harrison Center for the Arts in Indianapolis, US, freelancer Amy McAdams is paid half in money and half in sponsorship, which helps greatly with getting her name out into the community.

2 Ivancka Kroell calls this business card design a "love job" since it was for her mother's company. But as such, she says she could pour her energy into it and really let loose.

marianne scroope

kidsnkeys@worldonline.co.za
0828393881
100 high road, eastleigh, edenvale, 1609

2

"The freelancer has to be willing to make mistakes and accept them as part of the process."

Camillia BenBassat, Freelance designer, New York City, US

- Good people skills.

- The ability to be persuasive, perhaps a bit stubborn, but to know when to compromise.

- Be efficient and productive.

- Be able to deliver quality results within a reasonable timeframe.

- Have the ability and stamina to finish quickly and ask clients, "What's next?"

- Good organizational skills. This extends past the project into archiving and record-keeping.

- Understanding how the business world works and communicates.

- The ability to corral creativity in order to hit deadlines and meet budgets.

- The ability to "read" clients and appropriately personalize the service you provide.

- The ability to prioritize.

- Be objective and not overly emotionally attached to your work.

- Solid visual judgment, of one's own work as well as that of others.

The important thing when considering these factors is to not kid yourself. No one has every attribute on the list, but some items are not optional: if at your very core you are not a self-motivated person, then freelance design is not for you. If you know that criticism quenches your creative spark, you won't last a week. The same applies to an inability to listen or communicate clearly.

Other items on the list, however, can be learned and developed. Classes, mentors, experienced freelancers, books, and websites are great sources of information on business and networking skills in particular. We'll cover such skills in later chapters.

The switch to full-time freelance design will produce an enormous transformation in your life. It will absolutely not give you more free time or less stress—in fact, if you're successful, quite the opposite will be true. Your work will no longer be just a job with finite hours. Because of the intimate way in which you will be involved in every aspect of the development of your new venture, it will *become* your life.

1 Indianapolis–based designer Amy McAdams has the opportunity to produce beautiful work such as this poster for The Harrison Center for the Arts. Receiving half of her pay in sponsorship is a big help with her self-promotion.

1

"Talent gets the first-time customer; people skills and performance gets repeat customers."

Rodney Davidson, Freelance designer, Alabama, US

1 Freelancer Amy McAdams gave her client a version of this book cover that showed the image the client had in his head—a baby crying in the mirror—as well as a more "in your face" version. He preferred her idea.

Art direction: Amy McAdams and Matthew Hardy; author: Matthew Hardy

A Culture of Crybabies
The 21st Century World of Wimps, Whiners, and Victims

Matthew Hardy

WHAT IS YOUR PICTURE OF SUCCESS?

Because so much is at stake, it's crucial to take time to evaluate exactly what it is you want from your new life. Carefully answer the following questions. Use your answers to determine your short- and long-term life and business plans. There are no "right" answers—only answers that are right for you. Mark your calendar to revisit the questions and your answers every six months. Is your work keeping you on track toward your picture of success?

1   What are the five most important things in my life?

2   What are my greatest design strengths/skills?

3   What are my greatest business skills?

4   What are my greatest personal/people skills?

5   What talents do I have that are not being used now?

6   What specific things can I do with these skills to improve life for myself and others?

7   What sort of work has been the most satisfying for me in the past?

8   What sort of work has been the least satisfying?

9   How could I improve my skills?

10 How can I best allot my time to my friends, family, and myself?

11 If there were no restrictions on my time or finances, what would I do?

12 Which do I wish I had more of: time or money?

13 Are there things I really wish I were doing in my life?

14 What are the major roles I play in life?

15 Over the course of my lifetime, what are the most important goals for each of these roles?

16 How can I better match my personal values with my work?

17 Where do I want to be as a freelance designer in the next six months?

18 In two years?

19 In five years?

20 If I could change anything about my life, what would it be?

1

① Brooke Goans of Brooke Goans/Originals in Missouri, US, says that combining information in a functional and beautiful way sets her custom-designed invitations apart. *Printing: Witt Print Shop*

Should you be on your own?

This is a fundamental question, one that is closely tied to the necessary skills listed earlier. You may never hear tinkling bells or angelic voices telling you that the moment has arrived, but experienced freelancers report that there are signals.

"I knew I had to start freelancing when people started asking to work with me. A couple of clients approached me and asked me to do jobs for them. I knew it was the right time to make the switch," recalls Javier Escalante of Mexico City, Mexico, who was working for another firm at the time.

There's no tool to measure it, but a gut feeling that you have the necessary connections and clients in place will help new freelancers to sleep better at night. Consider whether you have a good business reputation outside of your role as an employee.

Recognizing that you don't need the imposed schedules and structure of an office to feel motivated can be another signal. One designer reported that while many other creatives in her previous office sat back and waited for the next project to roll in, she was always inquiring about what she could do next.

Another important factor is whether or not you are ready to present a united front to the world; in other words, you don't want to look as though your business is just something you do on the side. This is your full-time work: your personal appearance, office, portfolio, promotional materials, phone manner; everything must be in place and look the part.

Susanna Edwards, a freelancer in London, UK, says that having one's own product in place—that is, a set of design skills that are attractive to clients—is crucial. In addition, "You have to be a creative and a manager. You also need to reinvent and be aware of contemporary practices in the industry. You need to be comfortable with taking risks and commit for the long haul," she says.

Many freelancers also point out that the ability to say no is crucial. This can be in response to jobs that you don't want, or to friends or family who don't think you have a real job. Babysitting for "just a minute," running a few errands for someone, being the emergency "sick" contact for other people's kids: just because you manage your own schedule does not mean your time is not valuable or that you are always available.

Saying no also extends to sometimes turning down family, friends, or even clients when they ask for a free job. You have to be ready to fight your corner to defend the value of your work.

In addition to being honest about your pursuits with your family and friends, you also need to be honest with clients. If a customer is likely to hear your toddler talking in the background of a call, or if you need part of your day carved out to care for an older family member or pick up students, tell the client the truth about your situation. Likely it won't affect your relationship at all, and

"Don't work for yourself until you've worked with someone else first. You need to be in an environment where you can see how the creative directors and art directors and designers and vendors and everything else works together."

Lisa Sarkees, Freelance designer, San Diego, US

the client will appreciate knowing exactly when he or she can reach you for uninterrupted conversation. Unless you can offer seamless service, pretending that your one-person office is bigger or more fully staffed than it is leads to mistrust, because the truth usually comes out.

2 Many times a freelancer's first client is his last employer. When Pennsylvania-based designer L. Steven Pashley of LSP Interactive decided that a 90-minute commute was just too much, he decided to go out on his own—but not before asking if he could continue to work with his employer. Their relationship remains successful.
Site design for Spencers, Webline; creative direction, LSP

2

❶ Freelancers can create their own design opportunities. South African designer Ivancka Kroell frequently walks her dogs at a park that was sponsoring a fun day. She created, pro bono, invites for the organizers that also carried her contact information.

Should you be a generalist or a specialist?

There are three camps of opinion on this question: generalist, specialist, or neither/both. The best choice for you will make itself known over time, but here is some basic reasoning for each:

Generalist. "A cross-disciplinary approach helps the work go further creatively. I am constantly excited by the challenges of expanding on my current skill set. It's possible for me to work with many clients on many different sorts of projects."

Specialist. "My clients know that I am the best at what I do. This gives me a huge advantage over generalists, who sometimes turn out to know a little about a lot of things."

Neither/both. "It's not better to be one or the other. Making a living doing just one thing is rare nowadays, and freelancers who are generalists can't possibly do it all themselves or know everything they need to know. It's best to be a generalist with a few specialist skills or work with a certain category of clients; or, be a specialist but work with lots of different sorts of clients."

1

What will make you more attractive to clients?

Successful freelancers agree that the following traits will differentiate you from others:

- A sense of humor and being personable.

- Maturity and responsibility.

- Having a personal style.

- Not having a personal style.

- A willingness to follow through.

- Positivity and a can-do attitude.

- The ability to remain calm. Give the impression that everything is under control, even when it is not.

- Relevant and consistent self-promotion.

- Pricing your work appropriately for the market.

- Going beyond just knowing what the client does and really connecting with them.

- Demonstrating that you are working for the client, not just for yourself.

- Having plenty of accessible and reliable vendors with whom you have solid relationships and can call at a moment's notice.

turn yourself to the light...
and the shadows fall behind you.

Wishing You
A Happy Diwali
and
A Prosperous New Year

anu – prashant
c h a u h a n

2

2 Prashant Chauhan, who freelances under the name Zero 9 in Mumbai, India, believes that subtle and kindly self-promotions, such as this holiday greeting, create strong bonds with clients.

At the most basic level, the number one trait cited by freelancers is this: the ability to make clients' lives easier.

"If I can do that, clients will come back to me again and again," reports Jani Whiteside, a freelancer in California, US. "Show them that their goals are your goals."

"When you are getting started, the more generalist you are, the better. Just put 'designer' on your business card in the beginning."

Jens Mebes, Spincycle, New York City (by way of Stuttgart, London, Paris, and Los Angeles)

What are the daily challenges you will face?

"My challenges now are different from when I started," says Susanna Edwards. "The beginning is a bit like grabbing in the dark—who to contact, how, and what might be achieved. I spent a good four years just nonstop cold-calling and visiting people, finding out through word of mouth who to connect with. Now the daily challenges vary—juggling different projects at the same time, managing stress, knowing when to take time out, stop for lunch. Just fitting everything into the day."

Despite what many might believe, just going to work—no matter whether the office is at home or elsewhere—is a constant challenge for many freelancers. Without a boss or clock looming, it's tough to sit down and just get started. Distractions abound. Procrastination grows rampant. Staying focused is a real challenge.

Keeping up with one's own business is tough, too. When you spend all day working on other peoples' brochures or websites, the last thing most designers want to do is sit down and work on their own stuff. Record-keeping, billing, and other day-to-day office necessities also turn out to be some of the least favorite activities.

Isolation from others can also be difficult, especially if you're used to working in an office. "My cat just wasn't the same company. I even missed the weekly status meetings at my old company," Jani Whiteside says. She combats isolation with classes, regularly scheduled lunches with friends or clients, attending professional events, and even just taking her work to a local coffee shop for a change of scenery.

Freelancer Rodney Davidson says he always starts his day by going out to get coffee and his "people fix." "When I was younger, I was driven and reclusive," he says. "As I get older, connections with others become more and more important."

Other challenges include the following:

- Managing workflow—and, by extension, the flow of money. This is tough for most freelancers.

- Billing and other paperwork.

- Developing the organizational abilities that will make you a good businessperson.

"I had been dealing with burnout and projects that seemed to go on forever with no payments when I told my life coach that I just couldn't do this anymore. She said, 'You're right. You can't work the way you have been anymore. You have to find a way to do things differently.' She was completely right. You may love design, but sometimes you have to find different ways to do it."

Rodney Davidson, Dogstar, Alabama, US

1-**3** Freelancers have to seek their own fortunes. When Jill Anderson of Jill Lynn Design (based in Atlanta, US) began freelancing, she worked at a local bookstore, where she noticed that many self-published books were horribly designed. So she contacted authors and began designing new books, such as the three covers show here and overleaf.

1

2

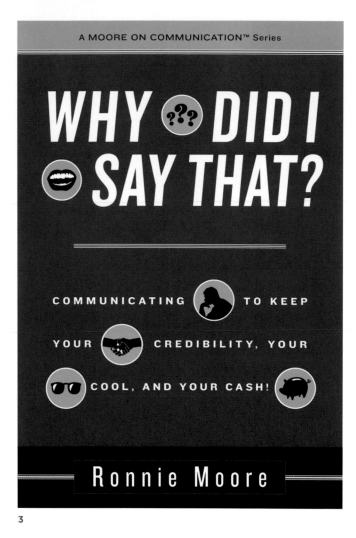

3

- Getting time off.

- Being accessible to clients 24/7.

- Insurance—obtaining it and affording it.

- Dealing with everyday frustrations, from computer failures to an overflowing trash can.

- The fluid nature of almost every job schedule.

"I am picky about the projects I choose. That makes it hard to know where the next paycheck is coming from. But I have to know the client or job is a good fit for what I want to do. Keep up the quality of the projects you do choose, and the work will come."

Lisa Sarkees, Freelance designer, San Diego, US

Case Study **Adam Hayes**

Adam Hayes has been in business for three years as a freelance designer with Penn Street Studio in London, UK. He moved into freelancing after completing a master's degree.

What makes a successful freelance graphic designer? The ability to adapt. I learned to do types of work I did not think I could do.

How do you know if you are suited to working on your own? You have to be confident in your own work. I have a business brain in addition to being creative. You need to be good at self-promotion and be friendly and approachable.

Is it better to be a generalist or a specialist? You have to be both. It's like asking if you want quality or quantity—most people want both. You do better if you can provide both.

How do you differentiate yourself? I don't really try to. I subscribe to the philosophy that "work makes work"—that's what attracts people. When I do free work for people, I will experiment with an entirely new style or type of work. Sometimes it's a style I can use in future, paying jobs, but it always produces a positive outlook for me.

1

What do clients want? Make contact with them. Build real relationships.

Challenges and surprises? People who start freelancing from their bedrooms find out quickly that they need more space. Getting clients to pay you for your work is always a challenge. You have to be quite bullish sometimes. Last year, I got myself an agent to keep track of payments and such. It is also easier to say no to projects the agent presents than to say no to clients.

"When you work in an office and there are slow times, you can relax. When you are freelancing and things are quiet, it means no work is coming in and the stress really gets quite severe. It's the exact opposite."
Adam Hayes

1–**3** A sampling of work from Adam Hayes, a freelance designer and illustrator working in London, UK. Previous page and left: cover design and illustration for *The Guardian* newspaper's *G2* section. Right: a cover for *ARC*, the journal of the Royal College of Art.

3

Case Study Seth Meierotto

Seth Meierotto moved straight into freelancing after college, then held a variety of jobs, not all design-related. After three years back in the freelance pool as BarkinSpider Studio in Green Bay, US, he has not looked back. "I'd rather haul lumber in a mosquito-infested, 100 degree, 90 percent humidity, no-breaks-until-something-breaks-sawmill than sit in a corporate cube again, thank you very much," he says.

1–**3** Work samples from Seth Meierotto of BarkinSpider Studio based in Green Bay, US. A trio of posters for Enzymatic Therapy made by combining royalty-free stock photographs in Photoshop.

What makes a successful freelance graphic designer? Creative skills are outside of the real needs. The more you know about marketing, the better. The more questions you ask, the better. There are lots of people who can design a piece of art, but there are fewer who can really communicate.

How do you know if you are suited to working on your own? You need to be a better designer than those in the agencies. You also have to be relentless; you will get a lot of rejections. Firms can be a little fearful of freelancers sometimes, and there may be clients who want to work with you but who don't

have time to stay in touch. You have to keep submitting stuff and keep your name out there. When I speak to college classes about showing your portfolio, I tell them that there might be a million people more talented than me out there—but I'm the one who is out there selling.

Daily, unrelenting challenges? It has to be educating people about copyright, contracts, and what they are paying for. You can lose clients if they are not educated or are not willing to be educated. Those people will just find someone else.

1

2

3

Case Study **Charlotte Fritzberg**

Charlotte Fritzberg is a freelancer working in London, UK. She recently left a position with Pentagram to begin her own venture.

1–**3** Samples of work from the portfolio of Charlotte Fritzberg of Blick Design, London, UK. Below and top right: a selection of materials for Cole Street, a café/gallery/design shop in Lübeck, Germany. Bottom right: packaging for the Green People line of hair care products (also including design by Suse Klingholz and art direction by Kasia Rust).

What are your personal goals? My aim is to work on projects that bear social and political meaning, while at the same time leaving space for aesthetics. Freelancing allows me to choose the projects I work on and decide how much time I dedicate to each project, which is very motivating as you are in charge of the progress you make.

Is it better to be a generalist or a specialist? I think a combination of the two is best. You need to have one area of expertise. This is what people often hire you for, but you still need to have some knowledge in other areas in order to stay flexible about the kind of projects you can take on.

Otherwise, you could end up working in one area and not getting out of it again.

What skills will you need? Project management, time and finance management, technical skills; but equally social skills, plus confidence. Even better, though, when presenting your work, that you have convinced yourself that the design will work.

Daily, unrelenting challenges? Timekeeping and getting ahead of the project are challenges. It is easy to get lost in the details. Attention to detail is important, but it can go too far. I usually keep a copy of the brief on my desk to remind myself of what it is I'm supposed to be doing.

1

2

3

Case Study **Bill Pandos**

Bill Pandos is a freelance graphic designer based in Athens, Greece. His work ranges from branding and packaging design through to magazine design and illustration.

1–**4** Work samples from Bill Pandos, a freelancer from Athens, Greece. Top right: cover and logo design for *In and About* magazine. Bottom right: identity for Lighthouse Design Studio. Following pages: poster design for Athens Fashion Week and poster design for Newcastle upon Tyne City Council.

What makes a successful freelance designer? Besides the education and technical skills, he must be able to find, contact, and maintain a list of clients—with their advantages and disadvantages—to stay in touch with those clients, and to design. He must also have the ability to keep records of everything he does during a project. He also has to maintain constant interest in what's happening around him, especially in his field of expertise.

What are your personal goals? First of all, I must have a balanced relationship between personal life and work. Neither should take valuable time from the other. Second, my goals are to have a significant list of clients and maintain them through professional behavior and attitude, and to provide them with the best possible results. Moreover, I want to educate my clients on what exactly it is that I do as a profession.

I hope at some point later to either be able to create my own design studio or teach at a university. I find it very important to be able at some point in your life to have the time and willingness to share on a more frequent basis all of the knowledge you have gathered.

How do you know if you are suited to working on your own? To make even a few initial steps, you must have patience and the willingness to succeed, no matter what the obstacles. And you must have the courage to take up on your shoulders whatever comes your way.

Is it better to be a generalist or a specialist? First you have to be a specialist. See what you like to do, then decide if you believe you can cover all of your expenses by doing only one type of design. Realistically, you have to be a generalist, too—a bit of a designer, a bit of an illustrator, a bit of a web designer.

1

What will differentiate you from the competition? Quality. Quality as a person, quality as a professional, quality in the designs you produce. You should also have the ability and willingness to offer your services for pro bono projects. Finally, you must be able to evaluate and follow your client's guidelines.

Daily, unrelenting challenges? You must be able to focus on what you are doing. Forget about the fridge and yesterday's birthday cake. Forget about noises from outside— people fighting, children playing, and so on.

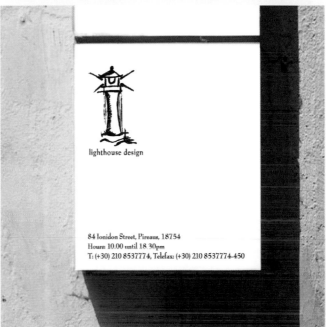

2

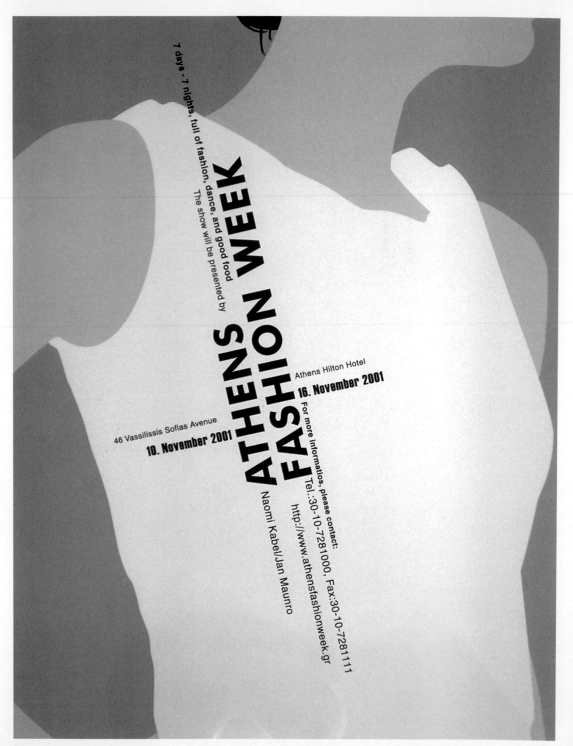

ATHENS FASHION WEEK

7 days - 7 nights, full of fashion, dance, and good food
The show will be presented by

46 Vassilissis Sofias Avenue
10. November 2001

Athens Hilton Hotel
16. November 2001

For more informatios, please contact:
Tel.:30-10-7281000, Fax.30-10-7281111
http://www.athensfashionweek.gr
Naomi Kabel/Jan Maunro

CONTEMPORARY ART JUNE-JULY 2002

EXHIBITION TOUR
(Thu 9 June-6.30pm)

with ANDREW BRACEY

ART STOP
(Sats 10.30am-12.30pm)

CREATIVE FUN FOR ALL THE FAMILY

BUMPS AND BABES ACTIVITIES
(Mons 6 June-3 July 10.30am-12.30pm)

With artist FLAVIA STONE

HOLIDAY WORKSHOPS
(Wed 15 June-Thur 16 June 10am-12.30pm)

with GILLIAN BAKER

MENTORING WITH FRANKO B
(Mon 20-Fri 24 June)

ARTISTS SURGERIES
(Tue 21 June 8am-4pm)

with KATHERINE WOOD

RAIL ROAD CROSSING

He often warned me that there were pickpockets in the crowd.

They fired some warning shots

2000 new railroad stop were positioned all over the country, after the Sardust, 2000 part we near the city of Newcastle, five days ago. Responsible for the placement of the new

WARNING

Sponsored by: Newcastle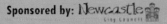
City Council

www.contemporary-art.co.uk
email: contemoraryart@newcastle.co.uk

Case Study Carly Franklin

Carly Franklin has been a freelance designer with her own company, CFX Creative, for eight years in Vancouver, Canada.

①&② Stationery systems for NALH Bookkeeping Services and BOOST Productivity designed by Carly H. Franklin, MGDC, of CFX Creative in Vancouver, Canada.

What makes a successful freelance designer? I think success means a balance of a lot of things—financial stability, industry and peer recognition of your work, and doing something you enjoy on your own terms (for the most part).

How do you know if you are suited to working on your own? There are a lot of hats to wear at any given time, so it's important to know when to seek outside help in areas that are not your strong suit. You have to be organized and good at scheduling all the tasks that need to get done so you don't spend all your time running around putting out fires as they pop up, all the while neglecting more important tasks.

Like lots of creatives, I'm a sporadic personality type, which doesn't always lend itself to adhering to a set schedule. It definitely helps to increase my productivity and efficiency when I am a bit more disciplined with my time.

Is it better to be a generalist or a specialist? As a marketing strategy, I think you definitely stand out more if you promote yourself as a specialist in a particular type of work. For me, this is especially true. I fell in love with logo and identity design a short time into my career and wanted to focus more on that type of work. When I started to attend local business networking events, I introduced myself as a graphic designer specializing in corporate identity work. In no time, I gained a reputation for that type of work and took on more new projects than ever before. In addition, though, a good specialist knows how to make sure prospects understand that they can address a wide range of design needs in addition to their niche.

Daily, unrelenting challenges? When you are in charge of everything, finding enough time to get all your whole to-do list done can be a challenge. Making time to market consistently is something a lot of people have a hard time doing. Managing cash flow to compensate for slower periods is also a challenge.

1

2

Hitting the Trail

How to Get Started

Alan had all his ducks in a row: an inspiring, quiet workspace; the right financing; a great list of clients for whom he had been freelancing on the side for months. His friends and family all agreed that he could make it in business for himself. He even had a logo and website done.

However, for reasons he could not understand, Alan had been unable to make that long walk to his employer's HR department and give his two weeks' notice. He felt frozen and—he hated to admit it—afraid. What if he couldn't make enough money as a freelancer to support his family? What if he never got a vacation again? What if... what if what? There were just so many unknowns. He felt like he could not go forward, but he could not possibly stay where he was.

1 Søren Severin created this poster for an open competition. Even though it did not win, Severin still believes that taking advantage of such opportunities is important. "Competitions are a nice way to control the entire process yourself and a great window to show work that is 100 percent your style," he says.

1

When should you make the leap?

Sure, you may know people who started freelancing overnight, without any more of a plan than what they might eat for breakfast. And there may be others who slid into it, gradually picking up more and more jobs until, finally, they were officially in business on their own.

But for every one of these people there is some element of fear, or at least worry. For most, it is the first time they have operated without the safety net of the salary, insurance, and peer group provided by their employer. Family and friends may or may not admire or support the decision to go freelance and add their own worries about your welfare.

The key is to get your own safety net in place, starting with a business plan.

What should a business plan contain?

A good business plan is indispensable to a busy freelancer. It is a touchstone that keeps track of goals and shows how to reach them.

"It's very important for me to narrow things down and have a vision of where I want to be in five years," says Javier Escalante, a freelancer in Monterey, Mexico. Otherwise, he adds, it's too easy to lose sight of why he went into freelancing in the first place.

Marga Ashley of Montreal, Canada, agrees. "Your plan should contain your goals for the next five years. You can add goals as you climb your way to the five-year mark. A business plan is a good tool to keep you on track and guide you through the rough patches," she says. "Of course, your plan can change as time goes on, but at the very least, you have a starting place and a finish line with markers along the path."

At its most basic, a business plan contains:

- Your mission: a definition of the business and what it does.

- Your vision: defined short-term and long-term business and financial goals. The goals must be specific, achievable, measurable, and time-based. They should present a clear picture of your future success.

- Your strategy: how you will achieve those goals.

Most freelancers will generate what could be called an internal plan: it is only for the eyes of the business owner. But if that owner seeks outside funding or wants to bring more people into the business, a more formal plan may be necessary. Business books and the internet are loaded with plan models, but any good business plan should have the following characteristics.

1 Designer Camillia BenBassat of Avec, in Brooklyn, US was able to effectively partner with a good friend for the identity of her new boutique. The shop owner provided her with plenty of creative freedom, and BenBassat offered her friend a reduced rate, which freed up monies for higher quality printing and letterpress printing, which benefited both.

"Freelancers definitely need drive. Because you are your only designer, your accounts payable person, you are the secretary, the scheduler, the agent, and more."

Alana Beall, Freelance designer, Maryland, US

- It must be written down.

- It should be practical and realistic, not wishful thinking. It needs to work for you.

- It is clear and concise enough to be read in less than 10 minutes.

- It is not carved in stone, but is not so fluid as to be meaningless. As new information and opportunities appear, you should be able to incorporate them into your plan.

- It must explain in practical terms how you will make money now and in the future, as well as how much money you would like to make.

- It should also include intangible goals, such as your definition of job satisfaction, your personal values, and your aspirations.

- It should contain guidelines for at least a year—ideally several years—that clearly state your goals, consider the competition, and acknowledge any risks you might incur (legal, financial, or emotional).

- It should contain a plan for what will happen if things don't go well, in addition to a solid definition of what "not well" is. This should include short-term plans (what if you don't get paid for a week?) and long-term plans (what happens if you become disabled and cannot work for an extended period?).

- It should re-energize you every time you read it.

Freelancer Marissa Strassel shares parts of her plan: "I have focused for the last few years on getting more clients in the 'green' and not-for-profit fields. I also set the goal of what I want to make in a year and analyze how I'm going to do that," she says. "I honestly don't look at the plan often. I did it quickly, and I didn't have anyone else review it. But it did make me go through that goal-setting exercise and find out what is really important to me. If I eventually want staff, what do I have to do to achieve that? I may discover that that goal is 10 years down the road for me, but at least I can see it is a doable goal. My plan is a roadmap for success on my terms."

PERSONALIZED BUSINESS PLAN

Chicago-based freelancer Marissa Strassel has created a personalized business plan, one that works for her. It shows the bigger picture while including plenty of detail.

Vision for studio
- Definition of my vision
- How will I achieve it?

Milestones and goals
- The current year in review
- The next year projected
- Long term goals (five years or more)
- Rough outline of ideas on how to get there

Capabilities
- Strategic communications (define)
- Print and website design (define)
- Potential services to offer (through subcontractor or through my firm)

Marketing plan/Networking ideas
- Key messages/Pitch speech
- Memberships
- Networking opportunities
- What sets me apart
- Competitors

List of collaborators
- Definition: other professionals in related fields that can either feed work to me or individuals offering skills I don't currently possess (i.e., Flash, SEO, etc.)
- Goal: to build relationships, team up on projects, undertake larger projects without having to hire staff, and have the potential to be exposed to a wider variety of projects (larger network feeding work to me)

List of clients
- Current
- Potential
- To target

Budget/Projections
- Personal salary targets
- Projection for future years (where I'd like to be)

Tax planning

Continued education opportunities/Training

Day in the life
- Description of a typical day
- Places to go or things to do if/when I get in a rut working alone

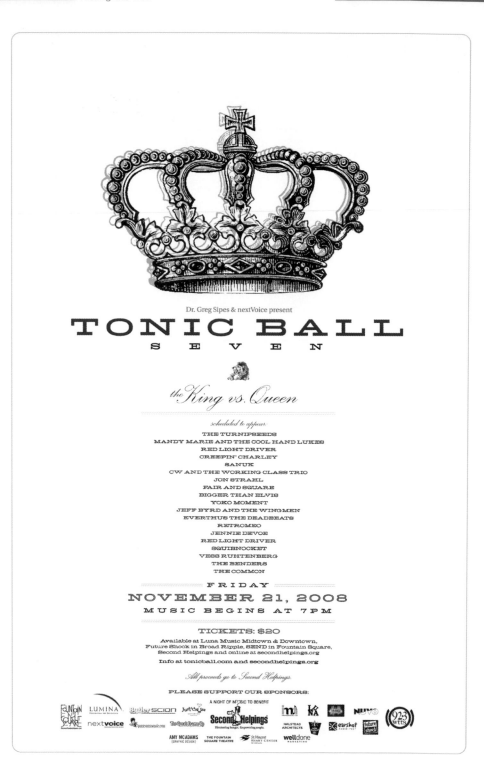

Dr. Greg Sipes & nextVoice present

TONIC BALL
SEVEN

the King vs. Queen

scheduled to appear:

THE TURNIPSEEDS
MANDY MARIE AND THE COOL HAND LUKES
RED LIGHT DRIVER
CREEPIN' CHARLEY
SANUK
CW AND THE WORKING CLASS TRIO
JON STRAHL
FAIR AND SQUARE
BIGGER THAN ELVIS
YOKO MOMENT
JEFF BYRD AND THE WINGMEN
EVERTHUS THE DEADBEATS
RETROMEO
JENNIE DEVOE
RED LIGHT DRIVER
SQUIBNOCKET
VESS RUHTENBERG
THE BENDERS
THE COMMON

FRIDAY
NOVEMBER 21, 2008
MUSIC BEGINS AT 7PM

TICKETS: $20

Available at Luna Music Midtown & Downtown,
Future Shock in Broad Ripple, SEND in Fountain Square,
Second Helpings and online at secondhelpings.org

Info at tonicball.com and secondhelpings.org

All proceeds go to Second Helpings.

PLEASE SUPPORT OUR SPONSORS:

1

Do you need a mentor?

"Especially in the beginning, you need a mentor, a person who has followed the same steps," says Bill Pandos. "He can be a professor, a professional from AIGA, or a colleague. The internet and its various forums are a good source."

A mentor can provide business and practical advice as well as inspiration. He or she could be a person you can meet and visit with, or a personal hero whose life and work inspires you from afar. A circle of designer friends can prove to be invaluable for immediate, face-to-face feedback.

Yomar Augusto, a Brazilian freelancer working in the Netherlands, relies on friends, especially those who are fellow designers. "I know their minds, their tastes, their styles," he says, which helps him understand their responses to his work.

Miq Reyes of Illinois, US, is big on blogs. "Every freelancer should have a blog or Twitter or something where you can publish your ideas. I follow other bloggers, too, then shoot off emails to ask if we can talk or collaborate. Freelancers can often be off in their own little world. Having others to talk with and leverage support from is huge."

Reyes also studies other design studios and will contact them for advice on business. "They are usually amazingly helpful. Most want to advance our profession and are not afraid to tell me how they work."

Finally, Reyes suggests going to conferences—design-related or not—in order to meet mentors. "There are so many people out there who can help you. Just picking one person [for a mentor] sets a bar that does not need to be there. Everybody is a mentor," he says.

Your workspace

Your choice is simple: in the home or outside of the home. But on one point, successful freelancers agree: no matter where your office space is, it should not be where you sleep or watch TV. If the office is in the home, it should be as separate as possible from your personal space. If it absolutely must be in a personal space, contrive a system where work and all of its trappings can be placed out of sight when you are not working.

① Pro-bono projects can be soul- and society-building. Amy McAdams of Indianapolis, US, creates design work each year for Tonic Ball, a local musical event where bands cover a chosen artist's catalog of music. It allows her to stretch her creative muscles and all proceeds from the event go to Second Helpings, a charity which redistributes prepared and perishable food among services that feed hungry people.

"Give big weight to office space. I put it off for three years and worked from home. Then I looked for a single office unit in an area of town I wanted and found out it was only $250 a month. I wish I'd done this three years ago! I work smarter while I'm here, it takes only a few hours of billable work to pay it off, and I've landed bigger and better clients."

Karen Chase, Freelance designer, Virginia, US

Other items on the wish list:

- Your office space should be clean with lots of light, including natural light for viewing color.

- Fresh air and a pleasant view are helpful.

- There should be a big desk or workspace with room for computers, peripherals, and stacks of work.

- Some designers like corkboards or other areas where they can post work and inspiration.

- Reserve space for a large calendar, timetable, or similar scheduling device.

- Bookshelves and/or covered storage help keep a space clean and well organized.

- Plan the space so that it is flexible enough to accommodate future media or jobs.

- Consider the conditions under which you work best. Do you like lots of noise and stimulation? Or do you need peace and quiet?

- Create the kind of space that inspires you. What color(s) give you energy? Is your chair comfortable? Do you have your music handy? Telephone? The degree of order and tidiness that you need?

- All office supplies—paper clips, scissors, tape, paper, and so on—need to belong to the workspace, not the household.

- Do you need to meet with clients in your workspace? If so, they can't be made to hike through living space to reach the meeting area.

- Do you want to share office space with another creative? An office mate can share costs, cover the phone while you're out, provide creative input and feedback, and be good company.

If you work at home, be sure that zoning and/or your building's rules allow it. This is particularly important if you expect to have package deliveries or clients visiting you during working hours.

It's also possible to maintain a hybrid workspace: work at home or in a dedicated office space, but get out whenever possible to take advantage of free wi-fi spots. The change of scenery can be a real tonic. One designer interviewed for this book says he even seeks out wi-fi spots in towns where he knows no one; it helps him focus on the work at hand, not on being social.

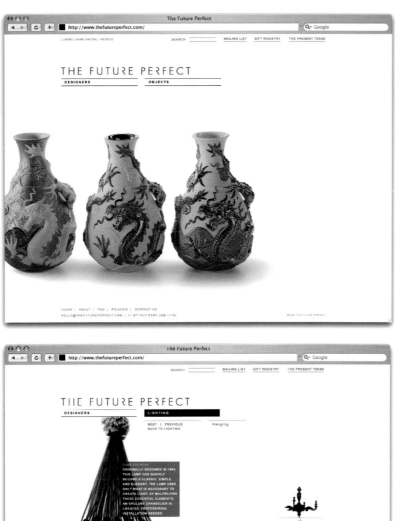

1 The Future Perfect is a unique furniture store in New York, very close to designer Camillia BenBassat's studio in Brooklyn. She met the client through simple connections in the neighborhood, helped produce this website, and is now working on in-store printed materials.

1

MICHELLE FA
JEWELRY

Michelle Fanta
and operated
roduce

MICHELLE FANTACI
JEWELRY

MICHELLE FAN

MICHELLEFAN

MICHELLEFA

What sort of bookkeeping help do you need?

At least while you are getting started, work with an accountant or bookkeeper who is well versed in accounting and tax issues for small businesses and sole proprietors. This person can teach you over time, and you can focus on your area of expertise: design.

On your own or with help, create a written budget for yourself. You may discover that you need fewer billable hours per week than you expect in order to make money and pay debts, and knowing where that profit point lies can definitely promote your mental health.

Multiplying that weekly "must-have" rate out into your complete financial year will also help you understand:

- How much vacation you can afford to take (remember that you won't be generating income during that time).

- What your equipment/travel/expense allowances are.

- How adjusting your hourly rate can affect your income.

Obtain a credit and/or debit card that is used exclusively for business purposes. It will make budgeting, expenses, and taxes much easier to track. A separate bank account for the business is also essential. See Chapter 3 for more information on the financial help you need.

What sort of legal help do you need?

There are many books and websites that make legal forms such as contracts available to designers. Chapter 4 of this book also shares legal advice that pertains to freelance graphic designers. But be aware that none of these sources provides specific legal information that you should act on. Instead, take your questions to a qualified business lawyer.

What follows are some general guidelines to consider when setting up your office:

- Visit a local business bureau to obtain information on zoning rules and area ordinances that might affect you.

- Seek the advice of other design offices in the area—large or small—and find out which issues are most likely to arise, and where they get their legal help.

- Go online and visit the chat rooms for informal advice. Make it a rule, though, to act only on legal advice given by a qualified professional.

1 When Camillia BenBassat was just starting her studio, she found another start-up, Michelle Fantaci Jewelry, to be the perfect client. "We are both start-up, small, creative businesses, and we have the opportunity to grow side by side," she says.

"The worst day here is better than the best day working in someone else's office."

Deana Corbin, Freelance designer, Illinois, US

①&② Even though this motion graphic assignment fell through, yielding no payment, its designer, Søren Severin, feels the job was not a waste. He learned a lot about motion graphics in the process and produced a nice portfolio piece. "Money isn't always the most important thing," he says.

1

2

What kind of boss will you be?

It's tough to be an ideal boss to yourself. Be too lenient, and your office will not flourish. Be too strict, and you'll never, ever get a day off. This is where a concrete business plan will help. The plan is objective, where you are not. If you have a set amount of income you must make in a week or month, it's simple to figure out how many hours you must work to accomplish that. Essentially, the plan is the boss.

When business is going well, be the kind of boss that recognizes your best employee for his or her achievements. When things aren't as smooth, sit down and figure out how to resolve it.

Brook Banham is a freelance shoe designer in San Francisco and his wife is a freelance graphic designer. They aim to make their work its own reward: "If you run a race and win, all of the effort is worth it. It's like that with our work. It's so satisfying to come up with a cool piece of art—it's like rewarding yourself. It's a blend of enjoyment and motivation," Banham says.

"You have to balance things, though. Once I have done something nice, I am out of here. We chill out and come back fresh— we work hard and play hard."

Montreal-based designer Marga Ashley suggests taking a personality test, the sort found on many job-search websites. "Answer the questions honestly," she advises. "Are you an aggressive person who likes to take charge, or are you the more laid-back artist who lets the designs do the talking? You are your company and you want to do yourself proud, so if there is an area you know you have to work on, be conscious of it when dealing with clients."

How will you name your business?

It is vital to choose a name for your enterprise. It must be unique and memorable, but it also needs to be registered as a business name for tax and liability reasons that protect you as an individual.

The most obvious choice of business name is your own name. This will represent you well and accurately; it is seldom like any other business name; it is often easier to remember than an impersonal name; and it is likely to be easier to register as a domain name and to search for on the internet. Using your own name also makes you seem more approachable.

However, you should consider choosing a name other than your own if any of the following factors apply to you:

■ There is someone else in the market with a similar name (related or not related to design).

■ Your name is especially difficult to spell or remember.

■ Your name misrepresents what you do (print designer Joe Webb, for example, should not name his office Webb Design) or otherwise casts an inaccurate or distracting light on the new business.

■ You believe your name will change in the future, thereby destroying any equity you had in the original business moniker.

■ You believe your business will grow into new iterations in the future. If so, just using your last name rather than your first and last name might work better.

Of course, designers are creative people, and a unique business name may have been in the back of your mind for years. The sky's the limit here, but with these caveats:

■ The domain for an original name must be available.

■ The name should explain what the business does (Kelly Design versus Kelly Inc.).

■ It is memorable but not silly or flip. You may only be working with local clients who know you well, but there may be larger corporate clients somewhere down the line.

■ The name needs to be flexible enough to expand with your business over time.

Seth Meierotto's last name is hard to spell, remember, and pronounce, so he decided to go with a completely new name for his business: BarkinSpider Design. In theory, it violates at least two of the rules of business naming: it does not indicate that he offers design services, and it sounds a bit light-hearted—and indeed it is.

"'Barkinspider' was a term my grandfather used to refer to kids in general or the sound of passing gas. I wanted a funny name—I was doing lots of caricatures and cartoons at the time—and there is nothing funnier than passing gas," Seth laughs. "Somewhere down the line, I thought that maybe I should

1 Karen Chase promotes her office, 224 Design in Virginia, US, religiously. Shown here is her self-promo book, which carries her brand color—Pantone 224. The other promotional materials she issues also follow a consistent style.

grow up and change the name. But no one ever complains. I meet with people in suits and ties, and when I explain the name, it just seems to endear them to the business. I do have a sense of humor associated with my business. If someone does not like the name, then that is probably someone I don't want to do business with."

Once you have decided on a name, sit on it for a few days or even a month, if you have the time. Then consider whether or not you still like it.

Announce yourself to the world

First, determine who in the world you want to contact. Develop several tiers of clients. The first tier will contain the most desirable clients. The second-tier clients may not be as desirable, but are still potentially profitable. Other tiers may also develop: pro bono work, new lines of business, new geographic areas, and so on. In the beginning, though, focus your efforts on the first tier, then the second.

There are numerous ways to announce your new business: self-promotional mail; a newsletter; a

website with emails heralding its opening; personal visits to clients' offices; a studio open house; a booth at a local business fair; advertising in newspapers or business publications. Associate yourself with a high-profile pro bono project in your area, or volunteer your services for a local not-for-profit business organization.

The method cited the most frequently by those interviewed for this book is simple word of mouth. Tell everyone you know: your family, friends, previous employers, fellow churchgoers, peers from membership or volunteer organizations—everyone. Even better, give everyone you know and trust two or more business cards (on quality paper— no cheap laser-printed cards) and ask them to pass them on to others who might be interested.

"There should be a good reason for your name as people will constantly ask you why you named it the way you did."

Charlotte Fritzberg, Freelance designer, London, UK

1

❶ Announcing yourself to the world can be an ongoing project. Lidia Varesco, a freelancer based in Chicago, US, sends out an e-newsletter to a select list of clients and prospective clients four times a year. "Solstice" shares news of Varesco's recent work, plus tips and resources for small businesses and a seasonal calendar of local events.

1

How do you establish good work habits?

For most freelancers, the problem is not a lack of hard work; it's working far too much. Especially with a home office, it's all too easy to send one more email or tweak a design a little bit longer until all of your free time is gone.

"You have to establish a good routine and stick with it," says Brazilian designer Eduardo Recife. "When I speak with most freelancers, the one thing they enjoy is the freedom they have to choose the time they want to start work and leave work. For me, the best option is to establish a time to arrive and to leave, just as if you worked in an agency or company. Otherwise, it leads to a very tricky situation where you don't know when it's time to rest and when it's time to work."

Establishing such rules as a start and stop time (or a regular lunch time, a predetermined week of vacation, or a set of holidays) forces you to focus on the work and the appropriate amount of time it should take—just as you would in an employer's office. Use traditional tools such as a planner or calendar to set the hours of your working day. Do the work in the order in which you prioritized it: if today is a design day and tomorrow is set aside for billing and making cold calls, stick with it. If you have given yourself the morning off in your calendar, stick with that.

If you are unable to police your own hours, bring in help. Set a predetermined, unmovable dinner hour with your family and promise to be there every day. Make appointments outside of the office (ideally for meals or recreation) at regular intervals.

Achieving a healthy work/life balance will be examined in more detail later in this book (see

Chapter 9). Understand, though, that the life of a freelancer can be chaotic. It's up to you to develop systems that make the best use of your time.

"My most successful projects have been when I have given myself the right amount of space," says one Chicago-based designer. "There's a lot to be said about the freedom and flexibility of freelancing, but be realistic with yourself about setting dedicated creative time just for designing. No phone and no email. Then put the work away and give yourself some more dedicated time the next day to just look at it again. It's a constant struggle to create that kind of time, but you have to do it."

Launch checklist

Are you ready to become a freelancer? Don't take the plunge until you have considered all of the following factors:

- You have a well-organized portfolio that will attract the kind of work that you really want. No matter how much you love them, don't include samples that are unrelated to your goals. Some designers choose to use a website rather than a traditional portfolio, but do have print work available if requested.

- You have a business name and a stationery system.

"I get all of the boring business stuff done in the morning. While I am doing that, I can't wait to get on to the sketching and fun stuff. The rest of the day is for creative work."

Brook Banham, Freelance designer, San Francisco, US

- You have a short- and long-term business plan.

- You have a well-outfitted workspace. Realize, however, that clients may ask you to work on-site occasionally, so be ready to take your show on the road.

- You have accounting help, legal help, and a mentor. In addition, have a bookkeeping system in your office that helps you keep track of paperwork and hours.

- You have a self-promotion plan for at least the first year.

- You have savings that will cover your business and living expenses for at least six months.

- You belong to a local design or business organization for networking opportunities. Even better, you have formed solid relationships with possible clients.

- You have learned as much as you possibly can about the clients on your call lists.

- You have spoken to friends and family to secure their support in your new venture.

❶ Organized by the Young Patrons of The Lincoln Center in New York, Tango on the Rocks was a fund-raising event that gave Brooklyn-based freelancer Camillia BenBassat an opportunity to work with a very high-profile client. It was a pro bono effort, but provided great samples and exposure.

- You have experience of running a small business or have taken a class or course to teach you these skills.

- You have discussed your plans with a successful businessperson in your area, with a local Chamber of Commerce or business incubator group, and with other designers.

- You have established a line of credit.

- You know the start-up costs for your business.

- You know you could get a business loan if you need it.

- You know how much money you must make every week, month, or year just to break even.

- You have established regular working hours for yourself.

- For tax purposes, you have established what sort of legal ownership works best for you.

- You have legal, accounting, tax, and financial planning help lined up.

- You know whether your business requires any special permits, licenses, or variances.

- You have a health and disability plan or insurance in place.

- You know who your core customers are and have a concrete plan for contacting them.

"How do you know when it's time to make the leap? When you believe that it's possible to survive doing what you like."
Yomar Augusto, Brazilian freelancedesigner currently working in the Netherlands

Money
Matters

How to Manage Your Finances

Lee could have sworn that he had checked the specs 20 times over before they went to press. But standing in his client's retail store, it was clear that the newly printed signs would not fit the frames for which they were intended. It was a nightmare: there was plenty of blame to pass around—everyone had signed off on the proofs—but he felt responsible. The entire pile of four-color signs would have to be reworked and reprinted, at his cost. Lee felt queasy when he remembered that his quarterly tax bill was sitting on his desk. His office rent was due next week. In fact, this job was going to pay the rent. But certainly not now.

The client—one of Lee's favorites—finally spoke. "I am so sorry about this, but we really need the signs replaced this week. Can you let me know when to expect them?"

When it comes to finances, freelance design can be just plain scary. Even with proper planning, cash flow can be irregular and unpredictable.

However, there are ways to reduce the worry. If you have the proper safeguards in place, unexpected events—a job gone awry, a hard-disk crash, a client who refuses to pay—should not prove fatal to your business or enthusiasm.

What you cost

The ideal transaction between the freelance designer and the client is one that is mutually beneficial: the client is satisfied with the job and is able to use the design to further his business, and the designer gets exactly the same benefits. Ideally, in a successful exchange, the designer gets another perk: the opportunity to be creatively satisfied.

But to make that happen, the designer must understand what he or she needs to earn in order for the business to stay afloat. That means generating a budget. Your budget should include the following:

- Overhead, including office rent or lease; necessary office supplies; hardware and software, especially when upgrades are anticipated; utility and communication expenses for the office space; ongoing education or training; unanticipated downtime of any kind, but especially for equipment

problems; anticipated downtime, such as vacations; insurance; security; self-promotion; professional memberships; and any other expense that is specific to your business.

- Taxes (sales and income).

- Regular outside services, such as legal or accounting help.

- Your salary.

By adding all of these factors together and extrapolating them for a specific period of time—ideally, a year—you will have an excellent picture of how much your work must earn in order for your business to remain viable. It will also help you decide whether you can afford to take on pro bono clients, for instance, or indeed whether you can afford to take a vacation, rent office space, or contribute to a retirement plan.

It's important to monitor all of these costs constantly. If a phone bill increases dramatically or a new software package is necessary, the total must be recalculated.

"Once I did a formal written budget, I determined that I only had to bill 15 hours a week to make my expenses. Talk about taking the pressure off! It also proved that I could take a full 10 to 15 hours a week to search for work when I needed to and still live a debt-free life."

Karen Chase, Freelance designer, Virginia, US

① In trade for her work as the graphic design of record for the Women's Chamber of Commerce in Nevada, US, freelance designer Sue Hoffman of Forest Hills, New York, has received a lifetime membership worth about $2,000, as well as multiple advertising opportunities and a seat at many events. The group also recommends her to other potential clients on a regular basis.

How to charge

The next issue to tackle is the manner in which your clients will be charged. The most common methods are:

- By the hour.
- By the day (or by another predetermined, longer-term time frame).
- By the project.

There are advantages and disadvantages to each method, and each job should be charged according to its specific requirements and characteristics.

Charge by the hour if:

- A project is simple enough for you to accurately assess its outcome and completion time (but do establish a minimum number of hours for those projects that don't take much time).

- A client wishes to be involved in a project to the degree that hourly billing may help police the amount of involvement and therefore the length of time the project takes.

- A client is clearly not sure of the solution or even the direction that is needed.

- A job requires a lot of sketching, research, or other "pre-work."

- A job is likely to involve a lot of meetings.

- Your experience with the client has proven that charging by the hour makes him more efficient in dealing with you—for instance, limiting phone calls, being better prepared for meetings, and so on.

- A client's accounting system requires that you provide an account of hours plus an hourly fee.

- It is common for that market segment. One designer notes that motion graphics or production houses usually expect a day rate, while advertising agencies prefer an hourly rate. Another designer says he charges design firms and ad agencies by the hour because they are more likely to ask for lots of revisions.

It's important to remember, though, that what you are selling is your creativity, experience, and business savvy, not just your time. Vendors sell time, while professional consultants provide much more value through their expertise.

A slight modification of the hourly rate is the daily rate, which is ideal for repeat projects or any job with which you are familiar enough to know that a day or two will be sufficient. A day rate also makes sense for those days when you are invited to work in the client's office.

2008
Alumni Program

THE THIRD ANNUAL
WOMEN'S HALL OF FAME

&

THE FIRST PIONEER AWARD

presented by the...

Women's Chamber of Commerce
of Nevada

"If I get a job that I have not done before, and I don't exactly know how to do it, I will not charge the client by the hour just because I don't have enough experience. I will inform the client that the job calls for some initial research and training on my part, and that it will affect the time needed for the job, but not necessarily the price. The client is expecting professional work, so if a job requires skills or know-how that I do not yet possess, I will not charge for my learning process."

Søren Severin, Freelance designer, Denmark

Charge by the project if:

■ You have worked on a very similar project before and know how long the job will take. This enables you to use your hourly rate to calculate a flat fee.

■ You are working on a long-term project. Break the project into stages and charge for each stage accordingly.

■ The client is more experienced in working with designers and knows the going rate for such a project. On the other hand, sometimes it makes sense to charge by the project when a client has little experience with design or designers. "When people aren't familiar with the design world, they really have no idea of how long a project will take, especially in the conceptual phases. [Pricing by the hour] makes these clients focus on when the job will be complete, instead of on its content or quality. Hourly pricing for them

only kicks in when change orders are requested," says Alana Beall of Maryland, US.

■ You need to refocus the client on the end result, not on how many hours you are spending on the job. However, when charging by the project, the designer needs to set a limit on the number of hours provided for the money. One designer interviewed said he worked on a logo for two years, with the client making revisions all the time. "I think it's reasonable to ask for the entire fee in 60 to 90 days—especially for a logo— even if the client is still thinking about it," he says.

■ A client's accounting system requires you to do so.

One caveat to bear in mind when offering a client a flat or package rate for a job is to be sure you spell out in writing exactly what will be delivered for that price. If you do this, the client knows what to expect for the money, and you will remember how much time to spend on the project.

When it's impossible to figure out exactly how much time a project will take or to simply offer a flat charge, opt for a hybrid: quote a single cost for the entire project that is based on an estimate of the total hours multiplied by your hourly rate. But let the client know that if the project goes beyond that amount, your hourly rate will kick in, although they would be informed of this switchover beforehand.

What to charge

When considering what to charge, start by factoring in your actual costs:

- Creative time spent on the project.

- Production and post-production time spent on the project.

- Other costs, such as printing, copywriting, or supplies—although it's often advisable to have the client billed directly for such items to eliminate your liability and prevent cash-flow problems. This means you will not be able to charge markups on third-party costs, but many clients require copies of receipts anyway and will not tolerate markups on outside services.

- Markups.

- Your costs (overhead, taxes, outside services, and your salary).

Experienced designers will realize that not all costs are neatly encapsulated by this list. "I always calculate at least 15 percent extra of the total cost for unforeseen time spent on revisions, late night work, and so on," explains Charlotte Fritzberg, a London-based freelancer. "It's also very important to carefully calculate the time spent on artwork, press checks, checking proofs, or simply organizing and managing the project—getting client approvals and organizing photo shoots, for example."

Fees and pricing are also affected by the geographic location of the client, the size of the client's business, its budget, and how the work will be used. Larger clients usually have larger budgets and larger implementation plans (the more the work is used, the more value it has)—hence, they will be charged more than a smaller client with the exact same project.

Clients who are not as familiar with design or its value may be more difficult. "One thing I've learned to be universally true is that the less a client wants to pay, the more they will demand. Understandably, the closer a person is to the money they are spending, the more they will want to try to squeeze out of their investment," says Carly Franklin, a freelancer and owner of her own business, CFX Creative in Vancouver, Canada. "Marketing yourself on price is a slippery slope: I will outright tell prospects if price is their main concern, I'm likely not a good match for them. Focusing on quality, and on setting your rates

"Pricing is a very personal topic for designers because many feel that what they charge for their work is directly related to their worth as a designer—or worse, as a person."

Carly Franklin, Freelance designer, Vancouver, Canada

1&2 Small projects can lead to much larger deals. On the right is a poster that freelance designer Jose Nieto of Square Zero created as a pro bono project for a writer's conference. It eventually brought him work from Penguin Books, a sample of which is shown on the far right.

1

so they are fair based on your experience, portfolio, and expertise, will ensure that you are not selling yourself short."

Franklin believes that raising rates can act as a filter for getting rid of less desirable, penny-pinching clients and lead to better projects. "Several years ago, I refined my market focus and positioning, and I saw a dramatic increase in business after raising my rates," she says.

"It's up to the freelancer to size up or pre-qualify the client. It's a powerful tool which we don't use often enough," says Rodney Davidson, a designer based in Alabama, US. "One troublesome

client affects all of the work we do for other clients. It is hard to do our best when we are frustrated and unhappy."

Freelancers can also take intangibles into account when pricing work: is the job fun? How much creative freedom will be afforded? Will it open doors to more work with the same client? Will the finished work be an excellent portfolio piece? Will the work be used widely and therefore attract more potential clients? "All of these things are often as important as the actual payment and can affect how much I will charge for the work," explains Søren Severin.

Finally, freelancers need to be aware of what the local market will bear. Books and reports issued by design associations can be helpful in finding this information, but the simplest way is to just ask other freelancers what their hourly rate is. Design publications and websites also publish salary surveys that may be helpful. Depending on your expertise or level of experience, your rates may not match perfectly, but at least you will know if your work is priced fairly for the market.

"I hardly ever lose a client on budget. But I do get nervous about pricing myself too high for a client. You just have to grit your teeth during the proposal and not be shy about charging for what you do."

Sue Hoffman, Freelance designer, Las Vegas, Nevada

1

Other fees and charges to consider

The fees and charges in the following list may not apply to every project, but they should all be considered for inclusion in your contract (see Chapter 4 for more on contracts). Make sure clients understand that these fees are in place.

- Printing, outside production, or other third-party services. These are often quite large bills, so it can be smart to make the client directly billable for them. If they are not, be certain to estimate these costs in your contract and spell out the fact that the client is responsible for them.

- Consultation fees. Time spent on educating your client should be compensated, likely on an hourly rate.

- Travel/out-of-office costs. Travel time is billable. Also, some freelancers add an extra fee if asked to work in the client's office rather than their own.

- Revision charges. A contract might include one or even two sets of revisions, but having an hourly revision charge for revisions beyond that may prevent the client from making petty or endless changes.

- Cancellation/rejection/kill fees. If a cancellation fee is written into the contract, the freelancer will at least get some compensation in the event that the client kills the project or gives it to someone else midstream. Make sure that such charges are assigned for each stage of the project, so that you can get paid no matter at what point the job ends. Alternatively, indicate in your contract the percentage of the original fee or estimated hourly cost that the client will be responsible for. Even better, obtain the cancellation fee (you may want to call it a "start-up fee") before any work begins and stress that it is nonrefundable. Also indicate to the client if you want to retain ownership of the materials produced thus far to

①–③ Adam Hansel of Deadvolt Designs in Tylstrup, Denmark, produces plenty of personal work—T-shirts and stickers, for instance—the sale of which helps support his freelancing. "Being a part of the art community helps to reinforce my individualism as a designer. It shows to clients that a good visual plan need not be stagnant and mainstream. Plus, I try to keep the Deadvolt art pieces as graphic as possible, so that present and future clients can find inspiration in them," he explains.

2

3

prevent the client from taking your idea and having someone else produce it (likely at a lower cost).

- Charges for sketches and preliminary work. Usually, designers retain this material. If the client wants it instead, a charge can be made.

- Rush fees. Be specific in defining what constitutes a "rush." Clients who are not familiar with design work and how long certain projects or stages take may have unrealistic expectations, so spell it out. Rush fees are also appropriate for clients who are well aware that they are asking for a schedule outside of the norm.

- Fees for final files. Freelancers are split on this issue. Some charge more for handing over the actual electronic files to a client, although this sector is shrinking. Many freelancers consider delivery of the electronic files to be part of the job. "I'd much rather have them use my files than have them ask somebody's nephew to recreate my work and leave out all of the detail that I worked so hard on," says one practical designer.

- Copyright purchase. This does not apply to every job, but if a client wants to purchase copyright or other rights for illustrations or any other component of the design, the freelancer can charge a set fee for relinquishing such rights. The Graphic Artists Guild's *Handbook of Pricing and Ethical Guidelines* indicates that fees for copyright purchase should begin at two times the original fee and increase from there. Find out first, though, whether the client really needs to own the work. "Most clients don't need to own copyright; they just want to be able to use it in the future. I rarely give a client the copyright. Instead, I offer the unlimited usage for a period of time which can be extended at reasonable rates," says designer Rodney Davidson.

When to charge

For long-term projects, interim payments can be very helpful for cash flow. Examine the project to see if there are logical stages at which you could bill. For example, a freelancer could bill after each of the following steps: research, ideation, artwork and layout, and printing/delivery. Be sure ahead of time that the client agrees to your system.

As all freelancers know, clients can drag their feet when it comes to payment. Consider adding a 30-day payment requirement statement to your invoice. If the bill is not paid in 30 days, add a percentage to the price and send a new invoice. Alternatively, offer a discount for expedited payments.

Save time by billing via email when you can, cc-ing yourself at the same time. Ask the client to acknowledge receipt of the email.

Bidding

For some projects—usually larger ones—clients release a request for proposal (RFP), which should contain every detail that a designer would need to complete the project. Be aware that other designers will receive the same RFP. It's worth asking how many others and who they are before you start the time-consuming process of formulating a proposal. If no answer is forthcoming, that alone may inform your decision. Also study the quality, organization, and level of detail in the request itself. It may offer clues to what working with the potential client might be like.

Find out, too, if the request for proposal is simply a cattle call where, for instance, 10 designers are being asked to create work for $500 each and the winner will receive an additional reward. This is an exploitative way for clients to research designers, and everyone loses. Even the chosen designer loses the $4,500 that was given out to the other designers.

Most often, however, the designer creates a design proposal that is submitted to the client. Again, the proposal outlines every aspect of the project, from the definition of the job, designer and client responsibilities, and services that will be offered, to the schedule, budget, and desired outcome. No detail is too small.

The Graphic Artists Guild's *Handbook of Pricing and Ethical Guidelines* contains excellent and reliable advice for producing an effective design proposal that, when signed, is a legally binding contract.

Anywhere you can provide a quantifiable figure, do so. How much will outside vendors cost? How many pieces will be printed? What are your fees?

With the schedule, set timelines for each stage of the process that you control; avoid dates, though. For instance, for a brochure, a schedule might indicate that you will need one week to design the piece once you receive art and text from the client. After the client gets back to you with feedback, it will take another week for you to prepare the piece for press. This type of scheduling puts the responsibility for client delays squarely in the client's lap, not yours.

"I absolutely love the freedom of working around life. So many people live to retire. I am living now."
Brooke Goans, Freelance designer, Missouri, US

1-**3** Lucky Trimmer Dance Performance was founded in early 2004 by two Berlin-based contemporary dancers. It provides an ongoing forum for dancers and choreographers to present short, experimental pieces on a simple stage, several times a year. Amy Stafford of Blixa6 in Berlin, Germany, has created an intriguing and smile-inducing series of performance postcards since the series' second show. Each card carries a photo of a child that somehow suggests movement or performance. Today, participants and fans are invited to submit their own childhood photos for use in advertising.

1

2

LUCKY TRIMMER
TANZ PERFORMANCE SERIE

1

numbers, and any other information that will help identify your work to the client's accounts department and speed your check back to you.

There are plenty of software packages on the market, including QuickBooks Pro, MYOB Business Essentials, and Peachtree Complete, to help you with this task. There are also plenty of classes available to help small-business owners become more adept at bookkeeping.

Set a regular schedule to keep your billings and receivables up to date. For instance, every month or half-month, set aside a half-day for invoices and another half-day for receivables so you don't constantly feel distracted by uncompleted paperwork. Those blocks of time must be inviolable.

Why not bill at the end of every job? This is why: because jobs don't end at regular intervals, which means billing is not at regular intervals, and incoming checks are also not coming in regularly. Bill at various stages in the project instead. Your billing schedule can actually help even out cash flow. It can help clients understand where they are in the budget, and they won't be landed with a huge bill at the end.

Billing and collection

There are three simple choices for handling your finances:

1. Find an accountant or a bookkeeper (the latter will be more affordable). While this is a cash-out-of-pocket option, it's usually affordable enough to be covered by less than a day's worth of billing a month (or you can set up a trade-out with a professional). A good accountant or bookkeeper is better able to see the big picture for your business and advise you for the future. In addition, preventing wear and tear on your mental health will help your business.

2. Do it yourself. If you keep accurate records, billing and collection can be quite simple. Each bill should state clearly the exact details of the job being charged, how much is being charged, purchase order or job

3. The third option is to handle some accounting tasks yourself but employ a professional for those that seem too overwhelming. For instance, a freelancer might use a

software package to keep track of all billing, expenses, and so on, but give the reports generated by the software to an accountant come tax time.

Ideas for smoothing out cash flow

- Ask specific clients if you can work on a retainer. The client may still require that you submit a list of hours worked, but you will at least have some money coming in on a regular basis.

- Pay yourself a preset amount every month (the amount can be figured out by creating an annual budget and/or by examining your income and expenses for the previous year), and recognize that your business income and your personal income are completely separate. Be strict with yourself: don't pay yourself more than the budget allows. If there is extra money at the end of the year, you may get a bonus, but don't bleed the business.

- Keep personal and business accounts completely separate. Many freelancers have a credit or debit card that is exclusively for business use. This makes keeping track of expenses simple, but be sure to pay off the credit card completely every month.

- Have a variety of clients—a few big clients, more medium-sized clients, and even more smaller

clients. To diversify your risk, make sure that all your clients are not in the same line of business or the same geographic area. Classify clients by the pace of their business: some may only have big projects at the end of the year, while others can give you business year-round.

- Sit down with larger clients and plan for the coming year. If they already know they will have a particular number of projects that need to be completed during the year, ask if a payment plan would be possible for the next 12 months.

- Get a good line of credit in case of a long dry spell. Shop around for favorable interest rates, and remember that a credit card costs nothing if you don't use it. When the next big check comes in, pay it off right away.

1&**2** Samples of the work of freelance designer and artist Maciej Hajnrich (aka Valp). Left: this exciting cover design for Pym Printing House emerged from personal experimentations. Below: "Trust the Future" is another of the artist's experimental efforts.
Photographer: Katja de Bruijn-Govorushchenko
www.iconogenic.com

2

1-**4** "Pay" can come in different forms. For the Vietnamese Film Festival poster (shown here on the right) freelancer Karolina Pluska of Warsaw, Poland, was paid in a conventional manner. But the movie schedule covers she created for the Center for Modern Art in Warsaw (shown overleaf) were pro bono jobs. Instead, she received monthly passes for all screenings, plus had the benefit of working with a very prestigious client.

Are you making money?

Knowing whether or not you are making money is more difficult than it sounds. Cash flow for freelancers is notoriously irregular, while bills are not. Each individual's situation will be completely different, but as a general rule, if you are able to save 10 to 15 percent of your incoming checks (or better) after expenses, including paying yourself, your business is viable.

Examine the following list and choose the monitoring methods that will work for you.

- Open a second bank account that is strictly for incoming payments. This is the account from which all business expenses should be paid. Keep at least three months' worth of expenses in this account, as clients can take this long to pay on larger accounts. Keep your personal/household accounts completely separate from your business account.

- Especially when you are starting out, employ an accountant to help with invoicing, sales tax, tax returns, and collections.

"Pay for as many business expenses as possible on one credit card. Even when that giant bill comes and requires a giant check, you now have someone else—the credit-card company—keeping track of all of your expenses. Then you can look at the money coming in and the giant check going out and know if you are making money."

Sue Hoffman, Freelance designer, Las Vegas, US

A professional can tell you almost at a glance whether you are making money.

- If you are handling printing or other expensive operations for clients, there may be a lot of money going in and out of your accounts. This makes it difficult to gauge your personal progress. Request that the client be billed directly for such expenses.

- Stay organized, even when things are terribly busy.

Planning for estimated/ scheduled taxes

Every country's tax scheme is different, so it's difficult to make generalizations. But most experienced freelancers have two simple words of advice: plan ahead. In Greece, freelancers must pay for health and retirement insurance every three months, while income tax is due every four months. In the US, freelancers are strongly encouraged to pay national and state income taxes quarterly.

Karen Chase has a somewhat painful although effective solution that guarantees tax money will be available at the proper time. "Take one half of every check you get and stick it in a savings account for your taxes. There will be money left over, and you can use that for donations, deductions, and big-ticket items for the business at year end for further tax write-offs," she says.

2

3

Another suggested method is this: "Sometimes I will move a large amount of money to a mutual fund that is liquid and will write my tax payments from there," explains Indianapolis–based freelancer Amy McAdams. "That way, when I'm banking, I don't see that money as income. It's tucked away where I don't touch it until I need it."

Can you afford trade-outs or pro bono jobs?

Most freelancers would say that they can't afford *not* to work pro bono, for the following reasons:

1. Psychologically, pro bono jobs are often more fun and therefore creatively revitalizing.

2. Pro bono jobs can offer high visibility, attract new clients, and build a better portfolio.

3. Pro bono jobs can offer great value in the form of trade-outs.

Choose pro bono projects carefully, making sure that they meet at least one or two of the above factors. Also talk to your accountant before assuming that pro bono or trade-out jobs will help reduce your tax burden: it is likely that they will not.

4

Trade-outs can provide fantastic deals for the clever freelancer, but make certain you get the exact terms of the deal in writing. State clearly in a written agreement that once the design work is completed, the client owes you his trade, no matter whether he actually uses the design work.

The following are just a few of the clever trade-outs submitted by freelancers interviewed for this book:

"A financial advisor traded my website design for financial advice, which saves me $300 a month,

and he's making me money by handling my retirement plan and stock/bond options."

"Sometimes I can get my logo added to a sponsor list and generate some free advertising."

"I have a few clients who I do trade-out work with—a record store and a clothing boutique. I love both stores' products. But trade-outs only work if you'd be spending your money with that client anyway."

"Ask if the client can trade-out for advertising or for a link on their website."

"With networking or business groups, and with trade associations, ask for a free membership or for admission to their events."

"I traded out a logo for a home security system."

"For a restaurant, I have gotten free meals and used their restaurant as a meeting place for nothing. That's great, because I can't have client meetings at my home office."

"You cannot deduct the value of pro bono projects from your taxes, unless it's a really big donation or a really big company. You have to just do it for the satisfaction."

Javier Escalante, Freelance designer, Mexico City, Mexico

Legal Considerations

Knowing the Law

The project started innocuously. Paulo had worked on dozens of logo projects before this one, and they all had a satisfactory outcome. He had met with the client to discern her needs, budget, and schedule, and started work right away. In the allotted time, he had created a logo with which both he and she were very pleased. But the check he had now been expecting for seven full months was not forthcoming, although the client was using his work. She had seemed so nice, so honest— why wouldn't she pay up? Would his contract hold up if he actually pursued the legal action he had already threatened? The issue was putting a dark cloud over his entire day, from morning to night.

DISCLAIMER: The advice offered in this book is for informational purposes only. Consult a legal professional for actionable advice.

The legal concerns of a savvy freelance graphic designer fall into three broad categories:

1. Determining the proper structure for the business.
2. Having the proper contracts and paperwork in place to protect you and your work.
3. Limiting liability.

It's impossible and unwise to offer legal advice in book form to freelance designers throughout the world. So, instead of examining specific laws or rules, this chapter will discuss the issues that all freelancers should be aware of. Research these issues to find out how they affect you and your specific circumstances. The chapter on Standard Contracts and Business Tools in the Graphic Artists Guild's *Guide to Pricing and Ethical Guidelines* offers excellent, straightforward advice.

Talk to peers for their advice, but do not act on it without the advice of a legal professional—hearsay provides an unsteady foundation for your business. Spending the money upfront to consult a lawyer when the business is set up will reap dividends later. Above all, look for ways to limit your liability.

Business structure

There are specific ways in which freelancers can organize their businesses. After taking income needs, risk tolerance, future plans, and tax considerations into account, a freelancer should speak with a lawyer or small-business expert for advice on which type of organization to select.

Be aware that certain countries, states, and even cities have special regulations regarding business status. Some require local business licenses or permits that indicate you are doing business under a specific name. Freelancers who take on clients outside of their immediate geographic area may have to obtain licenses or permits for those areas as well. Some countries require any small-business owner who is setting up shop to contact an accountant, who will register the office with the governmental taxing body. Other countries require your intent to establish a business under a certain name to be published in a local newspaper.

In other words, each business location will present a different scenario and to-do list. Consult a local business-development office, or even better, talk to a designer peer for advice: he or she has walked this path already.

For the purposes of discussion, this chapter will use business-structure names that have been determined by the Internal Revenue Service of the United States. The names of the business structures may be different where you live, but the

①&② Cecilia Melli, a freelance designer in Milan, Italy, served as Creative Director of *Coilhouse* magazine (shown below), published out of Los Angeles. That led to an opportunity to help redesign an Italian free press publication, *Urban Magazine* (shown on the right). She feels that perhaps being an Italian designer—or a designer from abroad in general—made her more attractive to the US client, which in turn opened the door to work on publications at home.

methods of organization are likely to be very similar. Study the advantages and disadvantages offered by each type of structure, and find the similar structure in your area that fits your needs.

Sole proprietorship

The definition of a sole proprietor is simple: anyone who owns an unincorporated business by him- or herself. This is the simplest structure: the owner may usually begin or end the business whenever he or she chooses, is in complete control of the business, and receives all income. However, sole proprietors have unlimited liability and are responsible for all debts

incurred by the business—a scary thought when large printing bills or other "floated" costs are considered. All income to the business is also taxable through the owner's personal taxes. There are also other, very specific, geographically-based tax and business advantages and disadvantages for this structure, depending on where you live. Consult a local small-business expert for detailed advice.

LLC Owners of LLCs, or limited liability companies, have limited personal liability for the debts and actions of the business group. The formation of an LLC requires filing specific paperwork and following government-mandated rules. One advantage of an LLC is that it can easily accommodate new partners in the future, but an LLC's lifespan is predetermined in the papers that must be filed.

S Corporation The choice to form an S Corporation is usually determined by tax laws. The income of an S Corporation is not taxed directly but is distributed among its shareholders, who declare their portion of the income on their personal tax returns. If there is a profit, the shareholder must pay him- or herself a reasonable wage. If not, the shareholder's personal tax liability is greatly reduced.

1

CONTRACT EMPLOYMENT

Another popular option for freelancers is contract employment. Many websites and organizations, including Coroflot, Aquent, Publicis, and Big Fish, match freelancers with clients, and some will even handle paperwork such as tax forms. Clients can also contact freelancers directly and bring them on board for a contractually determined time.

Whether you are considering signing on as a contract employee for a single project or an extended period, read the contract carefully and consult a lawyer before signing. Make sure you understand when and how your contract can be terminated; how, when, and how much you will be paid; whether you will be offered any benefits; whether you are covered by the client's liability insurance; how you can get out of the agreement, if you need to; confidentiality issues; and any other wrinkles that may later turn out to be crevasses.

Contracts

A contract may seem like overkill, especially for small jobs. But it's important to have things in writing, even if it's in the form of a purchase order that clearly states all of the parameters of the job. Even an oral agreement or phone assignment can be followed up with an email or letter from you to the client that restates everything that was discussed. Ask the client to reply with any reactions.

Some experienced designers simply will not work without a contract. If a client won't sign your contract, it's a clear danger sign.

"My advice to any new freelancer is to never agree to do any type of work without a contract in place—ever," says Carly Franklin, a freelancer working in Vancouver, Canada. "If a prospect hedges about signing a contract, consider it a huge red flag. Contracts exist to protect both parties, and there's no legitimate reason not to want to sign one. Sad as it may be, there are unscrupulous people out there. Without a contract in place, it leaves the designer vulnerable and makes it difficult to pursue matters further if it's necessary."

In addition, especially with new clients or those who have little experience working with designers, it makes sense to provide a copy of what might be called your "code of ethics," which spells out the rules of the game in straightforward language, and includes the responsibilities and rights of both the designer and the client. You can write this yourself, or you can use resources such as the Graphic Artists Guild's Code of Fair Practice. The Code, because it carries the weight of the Graphic Artists Guild, can give you more leverage in negotiations.

There are plenty of small-business contracts available on the web or in books for you to use as a model for your contracts. But don't use a contract blindly: ask a business lawyer to check it out first. Don't accept the boilerplate copy without

"Sometimes it can be easy to get carried away with a new project and start in before having protections in place. Although it's hard for me to not start brainstorming in the shower before I get a signature, I make sure to require 30 percent of the total fee as a deposit before I begin any actual work, unless I have a long relationship with the client."

Amy Stafford, Freelance designer, Berlin, Germany

careful consideration, either. You may have more specific concerns that need to be addressed, or want to include your code of ethics on the back.

Consider all eventualities carefully. You may want to declare your right to end a project prematurely if certain developments occur—for example, a schedule that has become so drawn out that it is interfering with other work, or if you become uncomfortable with the ethics or content of the project. Be very specific in your mandates: for instance, indicate that your office may withdraw from a project when it becomes inactive for 90 days and that you will notify the client by letter of your decision to do so.

Some designers insist that any deposits already paid or other payments remitted are nonrefundable and can't be applied to other, future projects in the event that the current project is canceled. If you or your peers get burned, or something untoward occurs that you haven't encountered before, update your contract so that you don't make the same mistake again.

❶ Created by freelancer Yomar Augusto for UNEP (the United Nations Environment Program), this poster carries a leaf-shaped running track that was meant to inspire youth to think about sports and nature.

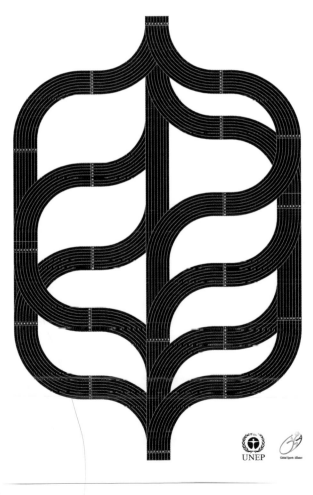

1

WHAT A CONTRACT SHOULD CONTAIN

All good contracts encapsulate a combination of needs, rights, and responsibilities. But you need to look out for yourself. Make sure your contracts contain the following information:

- Full name and address of the client and of the designer.
- Job title and a precise job description. Include the intention of the project as well as quantities, if appropriate.
- Your role in the project.
- Your estimate for the job, indicating that you will notify the client before the project goes over budget.
- The name of the person or people who will ultimately sign off on and give approval for each stage of the project.
- The name of the person or people with whom you will regularly communicate.
- Tax office information or reference number.
- The complete timetable, including all deadlines and a payment schedule.
- The amount of the payment or rate; a kill-fee schedule and how the kill fee will be charged—by percentage of work done, flat fee, etc.; rush fees; charges for revisions over a specified number; sales-tax issues; and details of how any other outside expenses will be handled. Sale of original art should be handled separately.
- The terms of the invoice. Are all balances due in 15 days? 30? State it here and on the invoice, too.
- Charges for loss or damage to files or art.
- It is possible to state in a contract that if the client wants to make changes to the artwork, he/she must ask the designer first.
- What you are expected to deliver at the end of the project and to whom.
- Who will be responsible for outside expenses, such as copywriting or printing. Indicate how time will be charged for meetings or travel.

- Copyright details. Spell out all rights and usages granted, as well as the estimated fee.
- Reservation of rights. This spells out which rights you have agreed to with the client and states that the designer retains the rest. "Legally, I could leave this off the contract as the laws leave all rights not given in writing to the artist," says one long-time designer. "But most people don't know that and I like to make sure it's clear upfront."
- Proper permissions. This lets the client know that he is responsible if he gives you a copyrighted image for a job but he does not have permission to use it.
- The credits you require on the work as well as how many copies of the finished product you will receive. Spell out the exact credit line you require.
- Anything that might limit future or current income opportunities (the client restricts you from working with any other real-estate agents in the area, for instance, or asks you to do an illustration that could be repurposed for further sales in the future). Put your wishes in writing.
- What will happen if the work is not delivered on time or according to expectations, including who will pay for legal fees.
- Contract termination, in the event that things do not go well between the designer and client. State the exact steps that are necessary to terminate the relationship. What fees will be incurred?
- *Force majeure*. French for "greater force," this is a common clause in contracts that frees both parties from liability or obligation when circumstances beyond anyone's control prevent a business deal from proceeding normally. A good example would be a natural disaster or loss of electrical power for a week. With this clause in place, the designer will not be held liable if he or she is unable to uphold the terms of the contract under such circumstances.
- Some designers include a warranty which promises that their work is original.

① This is a copy of the terms and conditions form that freelancer Ivancka Kroell (of Durban, South Africa) gives to clients, together with any quote. On acceptance of the quote, she requires that clients sign it and return a hard copy to her. She also makes sure that new clients put down a security deposit before she begins work.

"I have a signed contract for 20 book cover designs. In the contract draft, the client didn't mention what the titles were or when they would need them. So I put an expiry date on the contract: the 20 books will be done in a year. The contract will end after a year even if I have finished fewer than the 20 books, but I still get full payment."

Damang Chassianda, Freelance designer, Indonesia

Client contracts

Some clients, such as governmental bodies, require you to sign a contract as well. Read any client contract thoroughly and make sure it does not conflict with your own contract. For long-term, high-fee, or high-risk assignments, consider having a lawyer read it as well. Check the client out with the Better Business Bureau (or a similar agency) before you sign. And don't let a client-issued contract intimidate you—they are negotiable.

Stay away from blanket (or generic) contracts. Push for an agreement that covers the job at hand only. Also, a client contract should benefit both parties, not just the client, so make sure what is being requested is fair to you. Don't be afraid to negotiate or even reject the project, if necessary.

A common problem is when clients insist on retaining all rights; many are simply not aware that rights are a huge issue with designers. "Work for hire" clauses give the client all power over the freelancer's creative efforts, so it's best to steer clear of them whenever possible.

Compromise is sometimes necessary; for instance, you may not be able to hold on to long-term rights to the work, but you can negotiate that you hold on to your sketches and research.

"I'm not opposed to selling rights, but I am opposed to giving them away," says Seth Meierotto of BarkinSpider Studio in Green Bay, US. "A lot of clients don't know anything about rights and are using a canned contract. Educate them. Find out why they want all rights, and discuss whether they need them or not. After all, why should they pay the high premium for all rights if they don't need them?"

"In a contract, if you discuss doing three illustrations, there are just three, and not four or five. It's all about creating order. If they want more illustrations, then you can ask for more money."

Carolina Amaya, Freelance designer, Buenos Aires, Argentina

terms and conditions

Terms and Conditions

1.   Scope of work
1.1.   The scope of work is as per the above notes and subject to the same assumptions.
        Should the scope of work change in any way, this estimate is subject to revision and this additional work will not be
        undertaken until the Client has approved the revised estimate.

2.   Timesheets
2.1.   Hoochie Mamma will keep timesheets of all work undertaken on this project.
2.2.   Hoochie Mamma will advise the Client of time utilized on a weekly basis and will alert the Client should it become
        apparent that significantly more or less time will be needed to complete the work specified.

3.   Payment
3.1.   Clients are required to pay Hoochie Mamma as per the payment schedule outlined in the cost estimate above.
3.2.   Hoochie Mamma reserves the right to suspend work or withhold material should the Client be in breach of the payment
        schedule until such time as the Client rectifies the situation.

4.   Working hours
4.1.   One working day is considered as being eight (8) hours in duration.

5.   Confidentiality
5.1.   All work undertaken by Hoochie Mamma shall be confidential, until such time as the material becomes available in the
        public domain.
5.2.   The Client gives Hoochie Mamma permission to use this work in order to promote Hoochie Mamma (e.g. in a portfolio).

6.   Ownership of material
6.1.   All content created, written, edited, and managed by Hoochie Mamma remains the property of the client, unless
        otherwise negotiated in writing.
6.2.   The Client is to provide Hoochie Mamma with a copy of the final execution of work (e.g. advert, brochure, etc.) and
        allows Hoochie Mamma to use this for portfolio purposes, unless otherwise advised in writing by the Client.

7.   Cancellation
7.1.   Should the Client be unable to keep their commitment and the above project is cancelled or postponed indefinitely,
        the Client shall be liable to reimburse Hoochie Mamma in full for any work done up to that point (as per timesheet) by
        Hoochie Mamma, as well as an additional cancellation fee of 30% of the remaining value of the project

1

Limiting liability

The smartest thing any freelancer can do is to read everything, even the fine print, in anything he or she signs. State your abilities clearly and honestly. Never hide your limitations from clients.

"Sometimes young designers think that they must be capable of doing everything," says Damang Chassianda, a designer in Indonesia. "So they promote themselves much too high. It is pride at stake."

Ask plenty of questions. Get everything in writing and maintain a paper trail that tracks all correspondence, even phone calls. (To do this, follow up a phone interview with an email thanking the other party and restating everything that was discussed.)

Membership of design associations can also provide education and guidance. "In France, a particular association, La Maison des Artistes, can help you with law matters [such as] signing a contract," says Sally Targa, a freelancer working in the Netherlands.

Insurance can also help limit your liability. Consider every possible scenario. Would you lose your

"You are responsible for your own work. If you have done your part in a deal and you are still fleeced, then you have a way open to take legal action. But if you are stupid, then you can't expect a lawyer to help you."

Ruth Lance, Freelance designer, Darjeeling, India

❶ For one month, Yomar Augusto, a designer based in the Netherlands, was invited to display his work at an exhibition in Tokyo. The show resulted in new clients for Augusto.

house if you could not work for six months? Perhaps disability insurance would be a good idea. What if your office suffered a fire, or your hard drive fried, or someone was injured on your property? Speak with an insurance agent to make sure you have the correct coverage for all eventualities, including being held responsible for jobs that turn out to be disasters or clients who decide to sue. This is where having chosen the proper business structure can protect you; your business may be sued, but damages will not extend into your personal life.

Proper legal representation

Take the time to find a lawyer with whom you feel comfortable, before you need one—someone who is well-versed in business issues and whom you can afford. A business lawyer with intellectual property experience is ideal. Most freelancers never need a lawyer, but for day-to-day contractual or business issues (such as collections), it's good to have the weight of the law on your side. One freelancer interviewed for this book noted that every collection problem she has ever had has been easily solved by a letter from her lawyer that threatened further action. "It may cost me

$100," she says, "but it resolves the problem almost immediately."

Ask local printers, advertising agencies, design firms, and others involved in creative work to recommend lawyers who specialize in intellectual property issues.

Fair use

In order to maintain a portfolio and/or website, it's crucial to have what can be called "client comfort" with your showing the work you have produced for them. Even if all rights are sold to the client—say, in the case of an identity project—most clients will give you permission to display the work. This should be agreed in writing, either in a contract that is signed at the start of the project or in the form of a letter. The client may request special conditions—that you only put the work on your site after a certain date, for example.

If a client asks you to sign a non-disclosure agreement (NDA) at the start of a project that restricts you from ever using the work as part of your portfolio, consider charging more for the work. All client work has value to you, even after it is produced, as it builds the reputation of your company.

LAW IN FOREIGN COUNTRIES

Amy Stafford of Blixa6 is based in Berlin, Germany, but her job takes her to many other parts of the world. Here, she offers a sensible explanation of how she handles her legal issues.

"In my business, I work with clients and trademark issues that extend well outside the domain of the United States. Dealing with intellectual property issues is complicated enough in your home country and native language, but when you start crossing international boundaries things become exponentially more complicated. You have to consider that the kinds of laws you take for granted in your home country are not transferable to another country. The way the legal system is set up in Germany, for instance, is based on Book Law (what is written in the law books, typically by men who died many years ago), as opposed to US Case Law (making judgments based on what, if any, legal precedent has been set). From a sociological perspective, learning these things about a nation's legal system helps you to understand the unique psychology of another cultural system. However, it's typically more of a headache than fun, when trying to decipher arcane legal jargon in a foreign language where the words often have more than 20 letters in them.

"To help me wade through the bureaucratic jumble of German contract and trademark laws, I have developed a relationship with an attorney in Berlin who deals specifically with creative law in Europe—from advertising and graphic arts to fine arts, music, copyrights, and the constantly morphing world of digital-media law. An unexpected offshoot of this relationship has been that new client projects and referrals have actually spun out from it. In addition to getting legal advice, I have found myself fortunate enough to also get new work in the process.

"When I was first setting up my boilerplate contract and writing the clauses covering rights transfer and copyright use, I sat down with him to clarify the differences between the countries' laws and how best to protect my interests based on the different legal systems I would be working under. He has also helped me to understand how trademarking works in Germany and Europe and how it is different than in the US. When you consider issues like licensing a design or property, it is imperative that you discuss the details of your specific situation with a legal advisor who can help you navigate the copyright, patent, or trademark laws and local customs you are working within."

Sales tax

Sales taxes are not applicable in all countries. Even in countries that do have them, not everyone is entitled to charge sales tax, and those who do must file special paperwork in order to do so. Check with a local accountant for specific information.

Many freelancers interviewed for this book noted that if they email a finished job to a client, they do not have to charge sales tax. However, if they deliver any sort of tangible object, such as the same job on disc, they do have to charge sales tax.

Copyright and trademarks

Copyright law varies in every country and there is no magic bullet that protects your work worldwide. In addition, such laws are subject to change over time. A professional graphic design association in your area is a good place to start when looking for specific information.

To view a collection of approximately 100 national copyright and related rights legislation documents from UNESCO Member States, go to portal.unesco.org/culture/en/ev. php-URL_ID=14076&URL_DO=DO_TOPIC&URL_SECTION=201.html.

The World Intellectual Property Organization (WIPO) website at www.wipo.int is also very helpful. WIPO is an agency of the United

"If a client wants files without payment, forget that. Also never send open files, such as a .psd, until you are paid extra or it is agreed by contract."

Valp (Maciej Hajnrich), Freelance designer and illustrator, Katowice, Poland

Nations that is dedicated to developing an international intellectual property system that benefits the public interest while protecting artists' rights.

In addition, professional associations around the world monitor copyright and intellectual property legislation. Some, like the Graphic Artists Guild, publish excellent guides (such as *Pricing and Ethical Guidelines*) that no freelancer should be without.

Consult your peers. Post your questions on blogs frequented by other freelance designers. You may not get legally definitive, actionable advice, but you'll learn more about the issues and how others have dealt with them.

"Clients have come to expect digital files and sometimes feel betrayed when you try to charge for them. I have stopped trying for this extra fee for a few years now."

Sue Hoffman, Freelance designer, New York, US

Simplified usage and rights transfer

When your work will appear in different countries or you work with clients overseas, consider the following factors before you sign any contract:

- In how many media will the work be used? How many times? For how long?
- In what regions will it be seen (local, national, global, etc.)?
- Do you sell the completed work entirely to the client to have and use forever?
- Do you sell the client the rights to use the work for a limited period of time?
- Do you keep the original artwork or does the client own everything you create while working for them (work for hire)?
- If the client owns the work, do they have the right to modify it in any way they wish?
- Do you wish to be consulted before changes are made?

With answers to these questions in mind, you can build a set of copyright and usage terms that meet the needs of the specific project. In these terms, make sure you specify how the rights will be transferred, the category of use, the duration of use, quantity, media, geographic region, and so on.

Insurance

In addition to health and life insurance (remember that you are your business, and if you are ill or disabled, the business ceases to fuction), look into the following:

- Property insurance. This will protect you if someone is injured in your office; if the office is destroyed or damaged; and if business property is destroyed, damaged, or stolen.

- Interruption-of-business insurance. Whether it's a drastic event such as a natural disaster or a mundane occurrence like a power outage, interruption-of-business insurance could keep your office afloat until you can make new plans.

- Disability insurance. This will not replace all of your income, but it will provide some income in the event of a long-term disability.

- File backups. This is an insurance you provide for yourself, simply through proper planning. Back up all files—every day if possible, but every week at the very least. Keep a copy of the files off-site.

Proper personal ethics

While it may seem obvious, it is worth stating that there are some simple, ethical business practices that must always be followed: keep only licensed copies of software; have the proper permissions in place to use other peoples' work; declare income properly; deliver what is promised to clients; don't undercut on price; and deliver the best work you can using the best practices that you can. The reputation of the freelance graphic design profession must be protected by those who enjoy it.

1

❶ Yomar Augusto displays versatility in this calligraphy work for *MTV* magazine. It's a real contrast to some of his other work, which can be less "flowing." Freelancers who are able to produce a wide range of work are highly attractive to clients.

MTV art director: Beto Shibata

"The [best] legal protection for a freelancer is [when] the entire transaction is transparent."

Prashanth G., Freelance designer, Bangalore, India

Promoting Yourself

How to Get More Referrals

The previous month had been one of Jack's best. Work had flowed in at a slightly greater than manageable pace, but with a few extra hours here and there, all of the jobs had been completed and billed. Several were for new clients, and everyone seemed very happy with his work.

But now, after a weekend during which he had rewarded himself with two straight days of not working, the phone was silent. Nothing. It was always this way for him—feast or famine. It was as if he had no solid client base at all. Reluctantly, Jack pulled up his contacts list. It would be cold calls, all day.

It's ironic that so many freelance graphic designers, despite their expertise in promoting the goods and services of their clients, have such a hard time doing the same job for themselves. No time, no budget, no ideas, too many ideas, missed opportunities... the list probably sounds familiar. But ongoing, regular self-promotion is absolutely necessary for all freelancers, even when business is booming.

Consider that there are actually two different sorts of self-promotion:

1. Active. This is when you actively pursue new business.
2. Maintenance. This type of self promotion simply keeps your name out in front of people.

Also consider that any effective self-promotion should accomplish either one or both of the following:

- It should yield new clients or opportunities.

- It should provide information on clients or opportunities that you didn't have before.

If a self-promotional activity is simply fun, clever, or interesting, it's probably not a good use of your budget or time.

Conventional self-promotion

There are plenty of tried and true ways to promote yourself. Some conventional means include:

- Word of mouth. This is easily the best promotion a freelancer can have. Ask family, friends, neighbors, business associates, fellow organization members, and anyone else with whom you have a trusted relationship to spread the word about your business. Attend local and industry events in order to trade business cards. Ask vendors to recommend you to others.

- Direct snail mail. Bear in mind the general public's dislike of wasted resources and create a mailer that is either useful for recipients (a calendar, for example) or which delivers your message simply and in a thrifty manner (a postcard that directs the recipient to your website). Take the time to discover each recipient's name and title, if possible, to keep the message personal.

- Direct email. An email can deliver news or link the recipient to your website. Don't attach large files that are likely to be filtered out or not opened. Instead, paste a sample or two right into the body

"**I think the best promotion is your own work. If you do a great design, a lot of people will see it.**"
Sally Targa, Freelance web designer, the Netherlands

Eric Benoit | Boston Freelance Graphic Designer & Web Designer

http://www.ebenoit.com/

eric benoit - a freelance graphic & web designer   home   portfolio   services   about   contact

Want to squeeze the most out of your website?

Learn how to get your website to work for you.
By generating and tracking qualified leads.

Featured Website
Just launched, Smart Staffing Service has a professional website that displays their areas of staffing effectively. As a result of the redesign, their leads have risen beyond their expectations. There are some nice illustrations too.

View the website & details

Graphic Designer Bio
Boston based Freelance Graphic Designer offering creative services in advertising, logos and web site design. Currently employed at Hotwire Industries, a full service advertising agency, as a *Graphic & Web Designer*.

Learn more about me?

Creative Services
Services available but not limited to, logos, brochures, RSS Feeds, websites, internet advertising, search engine optimization and much more. Feel free to contact me to discuss your project, or submit a project proposal.

View services & descriptions

© 2008 Eric Benoit - *a freelance graphic & web designer*
Subscribe - Tutorials - Links - Sitemap - XHTML & CSS

1

1 Designer Eric Benoit of Boston, US, says that any freelancer who wants to succeed today must have a website for easy access. It is crucial, though, that any promotional site rank high in terms that potential clients are looking for. At the time of writing, typing "Boston freelance" into Google shows Benoit in the number two slot. "This is a big driver of business for me," he says.

of the email. Also, even if you are sending to a large email list, address the email to make it feel more personal.

- Website. This is a must in today's competitive atmosphere, even if it only contains recent samples of work and contact information. Naturally, the look and feel of your website should be a reflection of your work and identity. Keep file sizes small so that users with low bandwidth don't bail while downloading. Keep all platforms in mind.

You can work with an outside service to build and maintain your website, but do remember that if that person or company proves unreliable or uncooperative, your website is, in effect, shut down. Be sure that you have control of passwords and setup files at all times.

- Online portfolio. If you don't have time to create and feed your own website, take advantage of the many design community websites available which offer online portfolio space (see opposite page).

"The trick in such websites is to add as many tags as you can to your images, join groups, and add your pages to the image pools of these sites," says Minakshi Jena, a freelancer in New Delhi, India. "Post the URL provided to you with your profile on blogs and other sites." Also look into social networking sites such as LinkedIn.

PORTFOLIO SITES

Elance: www.elance.com
Coroflot: www.coroflot.com
CSS Mania: cssmania.com
Design Is Kinky: designiskinky.com
Flickr: www.flickr.com
deviantART: www.deviantart.com
Creative Hotlist: www.creativehotlist.com

- Cold calls. Most people's least favorite method, cold calls are nonetheless helpful, even if they only help you clean up your contact list or get a new address to which to direct mail. Research the client beforehand so that you can demonstrate that you have awareness of their recent design work and tastes. Follow up any cold call or office visit with a thank-you email or letter that contains all contact information, including your website address.

"Cold calls are the hardest," says freelancer Nanette Ferreri of New Jersey, US, "but even two calls per day makes a difference and makes me feel good, too."

- Competitions. Enter as many as you can, locally, nationally, and internationally. The visibility offered to winners is invaluable, and there can be other perks too. "I tried a French Adobe contest, which didn't take me long. I came in third, won some software, and a lot of people saw my work," says designer Sally Targa.

- Conventional advertising streams. Yellow Pages, newspapers, magazines—consider all of these as effective means of self-promotion.

- Classified advertisements. Check out Craigslist, Kijiji, Coroflot, MySpace, and other online direct-interest boards or forums.

- Pro bono work. This is often more interesting and inspiring than day-to-day client work, and the visibility it offers—and the cachet of appearing altruistic—is worth the effort. Ask the client for extra copies if it's a printed piece, and always try to get your credit line on the design.

- Pound the pavement. Put brochures and business cards in local stores, cafes, vendor offices, and elsewhere. Have a booth at a

---

"Where do you find people to promote to? Anywhere. In a bar, the supermarket, the elevator, in a bus or train, anywhere public. You just have to know when to talk and not stalk."

Michele Diaz, Freelancer designer, Chile

"Prepare and send a self-promotion. This is what differentiates you from your competition."

Bill Pandos, Freelance designer, Athens, Greece

① Self-promotions can be very personal and highly directed. For a photographer whose wife was expecting a baby, designer Kelly Hansen of Scooter Creative LC, Michigan, US, knit and felted a pair of baby clogs in her logo colors.

trade show where you have potential clients coming to you. Join the business associations that your clients belong to and don't miss a meeting.

- Be professionally connected. Freelancer Pau Ricart Masip originally worked in Barcelona, Spain, but has since moved to Ecuador. His experience has taught him that belonging to local design associations is imperative. Meetings and shows are good places to compare work and meet other professionals who might be able to help you later. Also become a member of local small-business associations.

Unconventional self-promotion

Freelance designers use all sorts of innovative methods to spread the word.

- Stickers, T-shirts, calendars, and cards. If clients, friends, or family are to wear your shirt or use your cards, they must have some other worth (wit, message, beauty, usefulness, and so on) than blatant self-promotion.

Adam Hansel, from Tylstrup, Denmark, loves T-shirts and makes plenty of them for self-promotion. "They are relatively inexpensive to

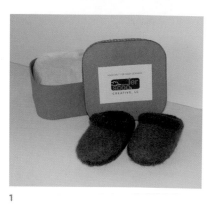

1

produce; they are constantly introducing you to new markets; and they show your versatility in modern trends, as well as your ability to start new trends," he says.

Designer Ange Luke—a freelancer from New Zealand who is now based in London—warns against gimmicky promotions: "That's what recent graduates do. So much of that goes right into the bin. When you have more experience, you need to show your work," she says.

- Visiting clients. Although not all clients are approachable in this way, Ange Luke keeps herself in the front of some clients' minds by asking them out for a coffee, beer, or lunch. "They may have heaps of freelancers, but if you are the proactive one, they will pick you," she says.

- Car signage. Indian designer Minakshi Jena highly recommends taking your message on the road.

2

- Newsletters, blogs, and other publications. Minakshi Jena likes to take advantage of regular publishing opportunities, but it's worth remembering that any publication or website you produce requires plenty of regular maintenance—try advertising your recent projects and offering business tips and ideas for clients. Online services are available that provide you with templates for newsletters, flow in your content, and even mail the newsletter to your client list.

- Group blog. Work with creative freelance friends to build a blog with lots of material and traffic. Lidia Varesco of Lidia Varesco Design in Chicago is part of a blog group at www.extrajumbo. net. "It's easier with eight people rather than just one. We do promo mailings together, too," she says.

- Mini-portfolio. Ivancka Kroel, a freelancer from Durban, South Africa, expanded her business card to a handy-sized foldout that includes samples of her work. "This has become a mini-portfolio for me," she says.

- Web banners. Partner with a client. You could consider giving them a discount for services in exchange for good placement.

2 "I received an e-mail from the company Pure Buttons which was offering free button packs to designers as a way to promote its new service. While I had never thought of creating my own buttons, I jumped on the chance," says Jill Anderson of Jill Lynn Design, Atlanta, US. One button describes the types of design she enjoys, while the other carries her personal mantra: Just Because You Can Doesn't Mean You Should. "Both packs have been a huge hit with potential and current clients," she adds.

1

1 Designer Ivancka Kroell of Durban, South Africa, uses this accordion-folded business card as a mini-portfolio. It's easy to carry in a pocket so she can have it ready at all times.

■ Instant Messaging. Although it shouldn't be the only method of self-promotion, there are moments when a quick shout-out to a client is a great reminder.

■ Tag-along. Elini Swengler, a freelancer in Baltimore, US, works with a printer who allows her to print her promos on the unused areas of press sheets. "These usually feature at least four or five images of new projects. I target the pieces to specific industries, rather than create a general promotion," she says.

■ Adult education. Swengler also takes MBA classes at a local college. All of her classmates are potential clients, and the business training helps her a great deal.

■ Write away. If you have writing talents, volunteer to produce articles for websites and local business publications that explain trends in design, for example, or which explain design principles to non-designers.

■ The surprise promo. Bill Pandos of Athens, Greece, suggests that on occasion a very special, one-of-a-kind promotion can be beneficial. For a Christmas gift for a client he wished to meet, he designed a beautiful wooden case and carefully placed inside a bottle of the potential client's favorite cognac, a cognac glass, and a well-designed holiday card. "The next day he called me to thank me and ask when we could arrange a meeting," he says.

- Freebies. Offer a downloadable calendar, screen wallpaper, customizable memo pad templates, or other free items that clients can retrieve from your website. At holiday times, offer downloadable gift tags or wrapping paper. Put contact information on everything.

- New "old" media. Designer Cinthy Revilla of Lima, Peru, reports that some restaurants and coffee shops now have postcard racks into which designers can place their own promotional cards. "Since the cards are free, everyone takes them," she says.

- Perceive the need. That's what Adrian Abdala, from Bahia Blanca, Argentina, did. "We can perceive inside our environment a lack of design. In my own city, there are more than 20 lines of

"Bring business cards along with you no matter where you go, be it a cocktail party or the convenience store."
Ronn Lee, Freelance designer from Singapore, now based in Shanghai, China

public transport. Whenever someone had to go to where they weren't accustomed, they needed to ask for schedules and so on, and this information was scanty and often erroneous. Having realized this need, I designed a free guide to public transport with all the information users needed. I gave them the design, people continue using this free service, and my name is known."

- Be yourself. Abdala also feels that even a letter of introduction can reflect a designer's way of seeing design and of working. He believes that sometimes designers are tempted to design according to the fashionable style of the day. All this does, he notes, is make the designer look like all the rest, not stand out.

"Remember that working freelance doesn't mean you work on your own. On the contrary, the freelance working environment is wide. Make friends with all kinds of people, as many as you can."
Damang Chassianda, Freelance designer, Indonesia

Think you've got nothing to crow about? Any of the following can be an excellent reason to send out a self-promotion:

- An award or other special recognition
- Completion of additional training
- Moving to a new location
- Completion of a project with a high-profile client
- Any holiday, large or small, including the client's birthday

Other promotional opportunities

- Stay in touch with previous clients. It's much easier to keep old clients happy than it is to go out and find new ones. In addition, satisfied clients are likely to recommend you to others.

- Be active online. Get involved with forums and blogs that relate to freelance design or even your clients' lines of work. On design sites, you can get honest feedback from peers on your work. Even just lurking yields plenty of ideas.

- Volunteer. Designers possess a valuable skill, one that plenty of community organizations want. Present yourself as a cheerful servant to other volunteers, and you are likely to get hired for pay jobs.

- Be searchable. If you have a website, make sure you are easily searchable, and include relevant keywords like "design," "web design," or whatever your specialty. Add your city or locale as well. Also, look into search engine optimization (SEO). There are plenty of websites, books, and professional consultants who can help you get more hits.

- Talk business. "I feel like my clients have responded best to less creative promotion," says freelancer Julie Bateman of Ontario, Canada. "They like it when you talk to them as a business owner, not as a 'creative.'"

- Go old style. London-based designer Maria Sletbakk Berge suggests that in the digital age, sending a paper promotion may garner a bit more attention.

- Get testimonials. Damang Chassianda of Indonesia suggests asking satisfied clients for a testimonial or evaluation of work you have done for them. Include these statements in your promos.

- Connect with other freelancers. The one-person machine sometimes needs help, and occasionally you may find a job forwarded to you if you have already built trust with other freelancers (and vice versa).

- Approach clients directly. Social networking can only take a designer so far; approaching attractive clients directly can be far more productive. For example,

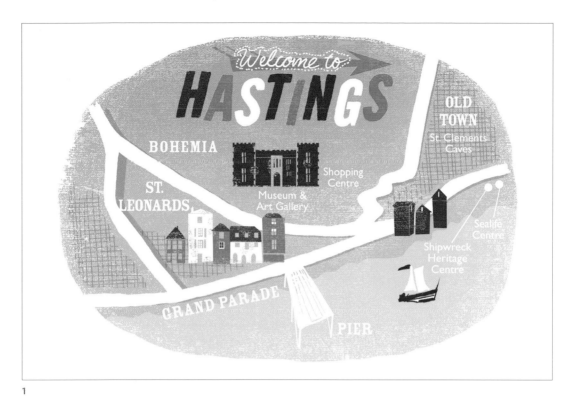

1

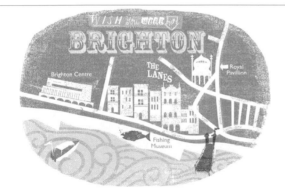

2

1 & 2 Freelance designer and artist Scott Jessop of Essex, England, advertises his illustrated map work with promotions that make perfect sense, considering the subject matter: postcards are sent to clients and potential clients that carry the phrase, "Wish you were here."

designer Michelle Diaz of Grafix in Chile, says that there has been a huge influx of Chinese businesspeople in her country. But most hotels, restaurants, and convention centers have no translated materials for these new visitors. "So I go to these companies and speak to their manager directly. I tell him that, as a designer, I have seen an increase of Chinese people visiting here," she says, adding that she can help them produce materials that provide guests with a positive international experience.

1&**2** Freelance artist and designer Carolina Amaya of Bogotá, Columbia, produces work for a wide range of clients. At left are two illustrations for Salvia Tea, and on the far left is a shampoo advert in which a woman's hair is made entirely of words.

2

Where do you find people to promote to?

There are mailing lists available for purchase, but for a freelance graphic designer, this scattershot approach can yield the wrong sort of clients. It is better to spend time building specific lists that fit your business and expertise. Again, trade shows and business association meetings are goldmines for making contacts.

What follows is a list of practical ideas shared by freelance graphic designers interviewed for this book.

- This sounds simple, but very few people actually do it. Look at groups who work in your field of interest, be it music, gardening, or whatever your hobby. Approach those people directly. For example, if you love art, why not contact galleries in your area and offer to design their next catalog? This way, you'll get to work on things that really interest you and even get paid. *Charlotte Fritzberg, London, UK*

- I use the *Business Journal*'s annual *Book of Lists*, which lists companies in major cities by industry.

- Check the design annuals to see which design firms and ad agencies are winning awards in your area. Sometimes they outsource work.

- I view job postings for designers to see which companies in my area hire creatives. I keep track of the ones I'm interested in, get the name of their creative director or marketing manager, and send an inquiry letter along with samples. Then I follow up in a week.

- I read the business sections of local papers to see what companies are growing or planning on moving to the area.

- I participate in several online design communities and have gotten a few clients by answering posts for freelance help there.

- If you are a specialist, attend conferences or trade shows for that industry. For example, if you focus on designing for the health-care industry, attend events geared toward doctors or other health-care providers. *Eleni Swengler, Baltimore, Maryland*

- Once I recognized a famous singer on an airline flight. I approached him to give him my card. I got nothing, but I always keep trying to find new clients with this direct approach. It is person-by-person work. *Yomar Augusto, the Netherlands*

"You constantly have to be on your toes. From dinner with friends to a phone call with a family member, every network is an opportunity. It is at times when I least expect it that I can make a long-term contact."

Nicole LaFave, Freelance designer, California, US

- Concentrate on having a long-time relationship with forums, online professional portfolio sites, and so on. Stay in them and be as active as you can. You need to keep your reputation out there.
Shoaib Ahmad, Pakistan

Should you work with a promotional agency or representative?

Working with a rep definitely has its advantages. "It makes it much easier to say 'no' to jobs I really don't want and still stay on good terms with the client," admits one designer. But it's an expensive option and, especially in the early days of a new freelance business, does not give you the face time needed to build strong relationships with clients.

But for some freelancers, especially those who can honestly say they are too busy to promote themselves, or are not good at promoting themselves, or when a freelancer is new in town (especially a big town), it's a useful option. The rep scouts out the job, knowing the freelancer's aptitudes, and the freelancer shows up to interview for a job that is likely to be suitable. Such agencies can also help coach freelancers on subjects like rates and lines of business. Some will handle all billing and taxes, and some will also help a freelancer find a permanent position.

Most agencies or reps ask for a commission or a percentage of

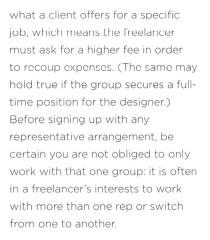

1

what a client offers for a specific job, which means the freelancer must ask for a higher fee in order to recoup expenses. (The same may hold true if the group secures a full-time position for the designer.) Before signing up with any representative arrangement, be certain you are not obliged to only work with that one group: it is often in a freelancer's interests to work with more than one rep or switch from one to another.

❶ Freelancers can create extremely far-reaching promotions, if they are alert. Freelance designer Adrian Abdala of Buenos Aires, Argentina, noticed that in his city there were more than 20 different lines of public transport, but no printed guide that helped travelers maneuver the systems. He created a free guide that carries his contact information, gave it to the transport system, and now his work is carried by thousands of people every day, taking his name everywhere.

"Hiring an agency may work in many countries, but in my region, one has to work as the salesman oneself. Your stack of art won't do anything until you leave your studio and act as a sales guy."

Shahud R. Shami, Freelance designer, Islamabad, Pakistan

1

1&**2** Holiday greetings are always a welcome change of pace for designers. At right is a New Year's promotion that freelancer Lisa Sarkees of Studio L in San Diego, US, made in collaboration with In to Ink Printing. For her studio's Halloween promotion, she used scrap paper left over from trimmings of the New Year's design to make pumpkins, which she filled with candy.

How can you get more referrals?

Start by doing great work, and then ask the clients who have benefited to recommend you to their friends and colleagues. Also ask friends and family to recommend you to their business associates. In fact, ask everyone you know to pass on the good word.

Keep in mind that when a client refers you to someone else, they are putting their own reputation on the line. If you don't perform well, they look bad. Not only does your design have to be excellent, you need to be responsive to phone and email, be pleasant, be a good partner every time, price competitively, and follow up. You might consider offering a discount or guarantee to woo in new referrals, or as a thank you to those who refer you.

Other ideas:

■ Create an incentive program that offers existing clients a discount when they give a referral that results in new business for you.

■ "Be blunt when looking for referrals. Tell your clients you are looking to take on new work, and that the best way you gain work is through referrals," says Eric Benoit, a freelancer in Boston, US. "My clients are my best sales team, and I don't even have to pay them."

■ To encourage clients to give you referrals, perform above and beyond the call of duty, says Kester Low, a freelancer in Kuala Lumpur, Malaysia. "That means, for example, delivering five options instead of the quoted three options, delivering on time if not earlier, professionally written emails and prompt replies, and being savvy in what your niche requires you to know."

■ Become known as the expert in a specific client field—for example, finance or health care. You will be operating in a smaller world, says freelancer Yuanita Prawira, but the clients in that field are very closely connected and are likely to recommend you to each other.

2

3 A great way to get wider exposure is to enter contests, as Carolina Amaya of Bogotá, Columbia, did for *Crann Magazine*. Her work won the competition and was published on the cover.

3

Selecting
Clients

How to Find the Right Clients

When he had first landed the client—his largest and most prestigious to date—Carlos could hardly believe his luck. He had accepted the project almost without thinking. The budget was fantastic and the schedule reasonable. When he spoke on the phone with his in-house contact, she kept telling him how pleased everyone was with his work. It was all incredibly encouraging.

Then a few face-to-face meetings with the client team went badly, ending up with them bickering among themselves and him sitting in embarrassed silence. Next came round after round of niggling changes, followed by repeated requests for overnight revisions. The retainer checks kept rolling in, but nine months later and no closer to a final design, he made a phone call he never dreamed he would make.

"Hi, Cecily? It's Carlos. Listen, I am so sorry, but I have to resign the account," he said, feeling much more relief than regret.

What is the right kind of client?

The answer to this question has two sides: a personal side and a business side. Of course, freelancers want to work with individuals who are decent and fair—and if they are fun and creatively inspiring, too, then that is the icing on the cake. Some designers choose to only work with clients who give them creative freedom; others can't afford to be that selective.

But choosing the right client also has a lot to do with finding the sort of work that suits you best, be it web design, book design, logo design, or whatever. Casting about indiscriminately and accepting any sort of work just to keep money coming in is a recipe for disenchantment and eventual exhaustion. Refer back to your short- and long-term business plans to make certain that any new clients fit into your big picture.

"When I first started my own thing," says freelancer Brett Yasko of Pittsburgh, US, "I would take just about any job because I was worried when the next job was going to come. Now, I simply ask myself, 'Is this something I want to spend my time on, and is this someone I want to spend my time with?'"

Every job has a personal side and a project side. Let's look at both.

Personal aspects

Every freelancer has his or her own standards, but there are specific client attributes that freelancers mention again and again. Consider your "must-have" client attributes and stick to your standards; write out a checklist if necessary. (For example, one long-time freelancer interviewed for this book described her "no jerk" policy: "I absolutely refuse to work with jerks anymore, no matter how good the money is," she says.)

- It's best if a client has some understanding of design and of working with designers, or is willing to learn. The client must also be able to explain the project well. "They respect collaboration but also your expertise," says Nathalie Bertin of Visual Funk! in Ontario, Canada.

- A good client knows what he or she wants as a result of the project, but does not try to

"Get them talking about themselves and their business. I'm interviewing them as much as they are interviewing me."

Tracie Valentino, Connecticut, US

micromanage the design process. "Tibor Kalman once said, 'Good clients are smarter than you.' A smart client is going to have good ideas, new ways of looking at something, and knowledge that I don't have. But he will also know that I am being hired to do something that he cannot do," explains Brett Yasko.

- The client must also understand that the freelancer is a businessperson and treat him or her with the same respect they would give to any other business associate.

- A good client has the patience to allow the designer to work through the proper process in order to achieve a good solution and not push to skip or rush steps.

- When it comes to revisions, a good client will offer valid feedback but not try to provide a new or modified solution—"Make it blue," for instance. "I used to

just go along with these changes since they are the client, but I realized that I am the expert. They come to me because I am the professional; this is the type of decision the designer needs to make for them," says Eric Benoit of Boston, US.

- A good client is decisive. On the other end of the scale is the time-waster: indecisive, disorganized, and ill-prepared. "[The best clients] do what they say they will do on time, whether it is getting back to you with information, giving feedback, answering questions, or paying the invoice," says UK-based freelancer Chris Robinson.

- A good client is also clearly interested in a long-term relationship.

Business aspects

"I believe we are in a commercial business," says Shahud R. Shami of Islamabad, Pakistan. "You have accepted this business as your bread and butter, so don't let opportunities go away just for the sake of creativity. It's always a mix. You are not a doctor in that you prescribe something and the patient will follow it."

The right sort of work

How do you find the sort of work that suits you?

"I had one guy who wanted an estimate for an ad. He wanted it cheap, fast, and to do it in trade. He just wants to fill up the space he has purchased and has no respect for the power of marketing and design. I don't ever work with these clients."

Kelly Hansen, Michigan, US

1

① Being a good friend can result in good work. Designer Chris Robinson of Crobbo Design landed this golf resort project from a referral he received from a friend for whom he did a free site. "Our relationship has gone from strength to strength, and I now receive regular work as a result," he says.

- Focus on what you do best. That said, it's also important to branch out and try new things—but be aware that initially such jobs will eat more time that could otherwise be used for earning money.

- Your gut instinct is usually correct. "The first face-to-face meeting will give you the most insight as to whether your skills are a good match for what the client is looking for, and it will give you your first impression of the client," explains Theraisa Fleig of Ontario, Canada. Be wary of clients who only want to converse by phone, instant messaging, or email in situations when a personal meeting is also an option. "There are some pretty clever and crafty scammers out there, so do as much research as you can about the client before signing on the dotted line."

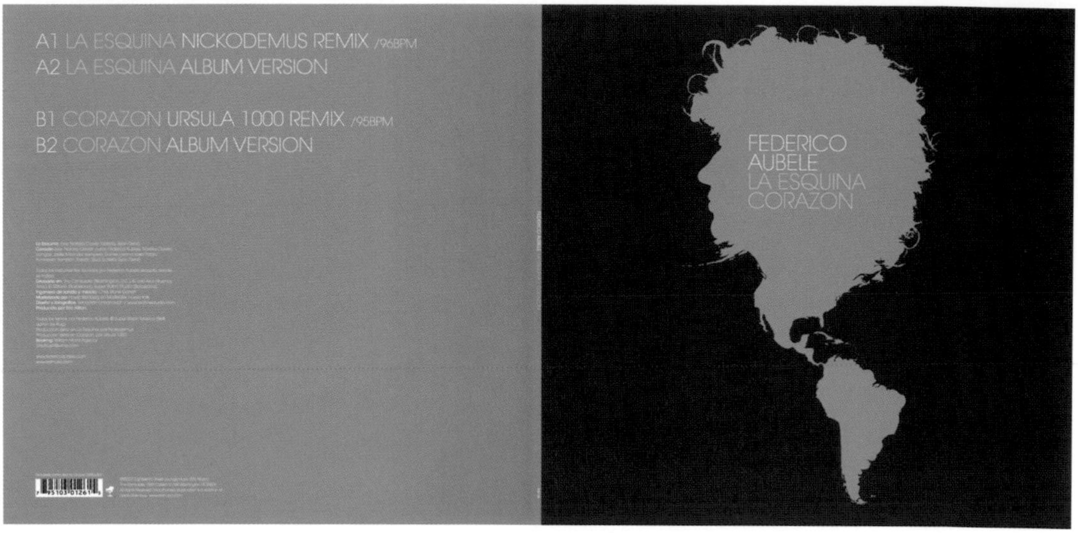

A1 LA ESQUINA NICKODEMUS REMIX /96BPM
A2 LA ESQUINA ALBUM VERSION

B1 CORAZON URSULA 1000 REMIX /95BPM
B2 CORAZON ALBUM VERSION

FEDERICO
AUBELE
LA ESQUINA
CORAZON

1

2

"The right kind of client is one that pays upfront, makes needs very clear upfront, requests minimal revisions, is incredibly trusting of your skills they are investing in, and never oversteps personal or professional boundaries... basically, a mythical creature like Superman or a unicorn."

Long-time freelance designer in the southern United States

❶&❷ TeaTime Studio designer Sebastián Litmanovich's work for musician Federico Aubele is mutually satisfying because the two are friends. Litmanovich was able to connect a photo he shot of Aubele for a press release into an intriguing illustration for the Panamericana theme.

Another danger sign is the client who wants to meet with the designer immediately, with little regard for your time, says Astrid Solis. "I do try to accommodate when someone is in a hurry, but this raises a red flag. This is someone who is not likely to have your schedule in mind. They want to be your only customer," she adds.

- Be wary of the client who freely shares stories about the long line of "ineffective" or otherwise troublesome designers he has already sacked. If the client has worked with different designers in the past, but the quality of the work has been consistently poor, the client may be a difficult one.

- The business should be able to pay a deposit or an upfront payment, if the freelancer requests it. If not, the designer weighs the risk of not being paid at all against the fun/ convenience/high-profile nature of the job. Another caution: if a client offers to pay the entire fee upfront, tread carefully. He or she may want you to put that project in front of all others or ask for other special or unreasonable favors.

- "Any client who wants you to change your contract for their benefit should be carefully considered," warns Nathalie Bertin. "The contract is there for your protection."

- Good clients don't issue veiled threats that suggest they can get the job done cheaper or faster by someone else.

- Sometimes a client will be highly likable, but his accounts-payable department will not be. "I've ditched several clients for this reason alone. Making me wait three to four months for money is definitely a deal-breaker," says Savyra Meyer, a freelancer based in Western Cape, South Africa. "Nothing is worth that kind of stress."

"It's not a good idea to sell your soul just because of the budget offered. Keep your ideals untouchable and your conscience clean."

Eduardo Recife, Freelance designer, Belo Horizonte, Brazil

How do you establish the right mix of clients?

Having the right mix of clients means balancing the amount of time available with income and job satisfaction. The proper mix will give you enough income and satisfaction through a reasonable amount of time allotted to work. If any one factor is out of balance, the other two will suffer: work too much and creativity dries up. Be purely creative and income is likely to recede. Work only for money and there is no time for anything else.

Achieving balance is easier said than done, since high satisfaction clients (pro bono, for instance) often pay little or nothing, and it's all too easy to pour way too much time into them. High-paying clients (such as a corporation) sometimes don't offer much creative freedom and such projects can be few and far between. And no single client should provide more than half of a freelancer's workload.

Achieving balance is a matter of compromise and of knowing what you need. When selecting clients, try to define them as follows:

- Small but mighty. These may not pay well or make the best use of your time, but they are either reliable providers of enormous satisfaction and/or exposure, or bear very steady (although smaller) projects.

- Mid-sized and steady. Such clients may not offer high-profile, exciting projects or pay especially well, but assignments and income are relatively steady or predictable. This category of client may offer retainers.

- Large but dry. There may not be much creative freedom, the meetings are long, and they have fewer projects to offer, but the pay and/or exposure is very good.

- One-timers. These clients will likely not be repeat customers, but they offer good rates of pay or high exposure. For instance, a local business organization with no budget may ask you to speak to its membership about design. You won't get paid for your time but you will have the opportunity to meet many potential clients. Or, a corporation with an impossible schedule calls you in for extra in-house help and is willing to pay dearly for it.

Clearly, the successful freelancer needs a mix of all of these types. Too many small clients, and income is paltry. Too many mid-sized clients, and the work may be dull. Having only one or two large clients increases risk; if one or both disappear, income drops dramatically. One-timers simply don't provide enough of anything to sustain a successful business. Create a mix that works for you and which balances your risk.

① The Iori Hotel project was especially satisfying for Barcelona–based designer Sebastián Litmanovich because the client allowed him to develop everything from the naming to all final designs.

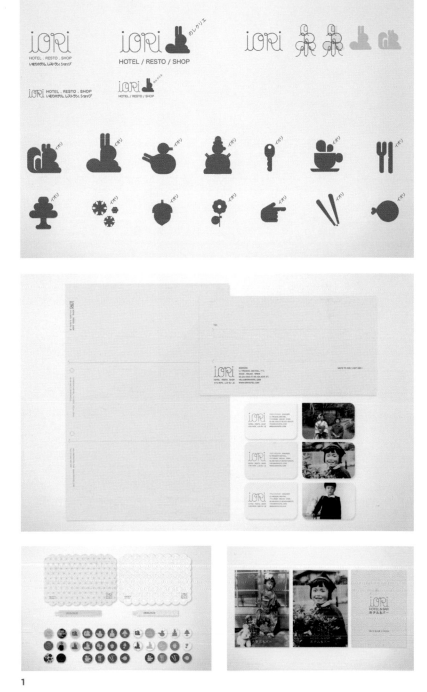

1

1

> **"Make a plan, write it down, and then figure out how to get there."**
>
> *Amy McAdams, Freelance designer, Indianapolis, US*

1&2 The Nike Shox Reveal project was an ideal one for New York–based freelancer Jens Mebes. What the client really wanted was for the designer to play with and explore the visual language, and develop a fantastical story that presents the produce in a very unusual way.

What do clients want from freelancers?

In general, it's safe to assume a client hires a freelancer because the client likes the designer's style or previous work. And while familiarity and security are definitely part of the hiring equation, clients also want to be pleasantly surprised. At the same time, they want the freelancer to have a thorough understanding of his business and show genuine interest in it.

"Clients want someone whose tastes they trust," says Tracie Valentino, who works in the greater New York City area. "I have one client who says, 'OK, we need a magazine ad. Here's the photography, here's the copy. Now give it the Tracie touch.' They know what to expect. They can give vague direction like that and know they will be thrilled with the outcome."

"One of the things that clients want is originality. To offer them a design that makes them different from the competition is indispensable," explains Adrian Abdala of Argentina.

Professionalism and respect are also crucial, in terms of personal relations, project execution, and organization. It's the designer's expected role to be the master of the software, process, and other tools that guide the design. An experienced freelancer can offer media opportunities a client may never have considered—outdoor advertising, for instance. Crucially, you must offer solid design at an affordable price.

Clients also want honesty; they simply do not have time to deal with anything else. This includes being straightforward about the design skills you can offer as well as giving direct—but not blunt—feedback on the client's not-so-great ideas. If a client's idea will be a waste of time or money, speak up (but kindly).

A client may decide to hire a freelancer over a design firm simply because the freelancer offers more flexibility in terms of scheduling, speed of response, and concept generation. The client is not separated from the work by a layer of other people, as he might be at a larger firm—receptionist, account executive, or project manager, for instance. He wants to work directly with one person.

"Clients want someone to listen to them and give them a solution. If you can deliver those two things with a smile, you'll be golden. If you do that and the client still isn't happy, you know that it's time to move on."

Amy McAdams, Indianapolis, US

Freelancers are often used to working cooperatively with a wide range of other freelancers in related fields (writers, web coders, print

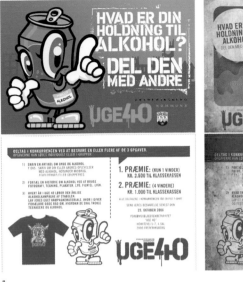

1 Danish freelancer Adam Hansel designed these pieces for Uge40, an alcohol education campaign organized by a local government. He felt strongly that supplying the pro bono work helped support the free campaign's reach and success.

1

brokers, and so on) while design firms may not be keen on bringing in other people from outside. Having a solid network of peers can be a real selling point.

"I think clients are looking for less ego," says Amy McAdams of Indianapolis. "New clients say they are intimidated by the big agencies and don't think they are the right fit for a small- to mid-sized company." Ironically, she adds, many large agencies and design firms hire freelance graphic designers to make sure they provide diverse, fresh looks for their clients.

Clients want freelance designers who are proactive and self-motivated. The last thing a client wants to do, says Lisa Sarkees of San Diego, US, "is manage me along. If I can take the lead to make things happen, the process is

smoother, more efficient, and on time and budget, which is good for everyone."

Sometimes clients want "a kick in the butt to get the job done," says Kelly Hansen of Michigan, US. "They are so busy running their business and would not get the design work done unless I was calling them every day—here is your copy, we are coming over to take pictures, whatever. We help them move their business along."

Follow-up in general is always appreciated: maybe the client just forgot that the last set of proofs is in his office. But sometimes follow-ups let the client off the hook.

"If a client likes the work, they will tell you right away," says Astrid Solis of Colorado, US. "If a client does not like a design, they may not

"The main reason I decided to work as a freelancer was to have the freedom to choose the right client. I don't like to work for big business because sometimes the work is so boring and not creative. But with small clients, I spend so much time teaching them how I work, what they really need, and why they need graphics—but they do give you more freedom."

Freelance designer in Ecuador

want to tell you. Or maybe they are getting a whole lot of feedback in their office, which also isn't good. They feel bad about calling you. If I don't hear anything, I'll just give them a quick call and let them off the hook."

Another general rule is that larger corporate clients generally want designers to execute their existing vision, or the established brand personality, but in fresh ways. They may have their own in-house departments and need only a specific service that is a small part of a much bigger picture.

Smaller and less established clients, on the other hand, are usually more open to experimentation. They may also want more generalized service and more consultation.

Understanding exactly what a client wants is vital for ongoing relationships, even when their desires go against convention. Tiffany Chua, a freelancer from Melbourne, Australia, notes that while the designer is intent on providing high-quality work, the

client might want something else. "Providing high quality work is time-consuming, while the client might need the job done quickly and is alright with compromising quality or style," she says. Speed may be far more valued than perfectionism.

It's also important to be compassionate and understand that some clients really don't know what they want. They may be too close to what they do, or want to copy what others have done. Perhaps they have lost touch with their own clients. That's when a freelance designer can provide a cold eye and help provide new insights.

Negotiating client politics

Anyone who has ever worked in an office with other people knows what a minefield it can be. Every client office is simply a collection of individuals, each of whom has his or her own agenda, difficulties, talents, and tastes. Every client has its quota of office politics. The freelancer has the unenviable task of sizing up all of these personalities each time a new relationship begins.

But there are ways to navigate this successfully. First and foremost, at the risk of sounding Pollyanna-ish, be nice. There's no defense like a kind smile, a sincere handshake, and a good attitude to make clients think twice about mistreating you.

Savyra Meyer of Western Cape, South Africa, believes that it is crucial to view clients with humor, love, and compassion, especially regarding the fear and tension so many office-bound people have in their lives. "It may sound soppy to speak of working from a platform of love, but very often one needs to see past the brusque communication and see the worried person behind the snappy, crisp voice," she says.

For an initial meeting, try to meet at the client's office so you can get a feel for the office, its culture, and its climate. The general condition of the rooms—messy, bare, streamlined, outdated, or completely up-to-date—will give you a glimpse into the psyche and aesthetic of the business owner.

In meetings with clients, notice who makes the most comments or seems to be the leader of the group. Whose opinions are taken seriously? Note on emails who responds quickly and who never answers. Who makes things happen and spurs others into action? If there is clearly an established leader in the group who knows what he or she wants, try to work with that person. Find out who the ultimate "higher up" is and get him or her into meetings, especially when big decisions are to be made.

Get *everything* in writing. Keep a record of telephone conversations by typing your notes. Follow up meetings and even handshakes with an email that acknowledges what transpired.

Before starting work with a new client, research them as much as possible. Ask other designers what they know, or check in with vendors such as printers for their opinions. They will be able to tell you who rules within a specific office as well as any people or pitfalls to avoid. Peers and friends may also help you find an advocate in the office who is more likely than others to champion design in general and your work specifically.

Also be certain that the client's expectations are realistic and match yours. Much of this can be handled through your contracts, but the person who signs your document may not be the same person who signs your checks, and those two people may never speak at all. Company policy out-trumps all, and your puny "30 days past due" statement will mean nothing to an organization who only pays every 90 days.

It also makes sense to check in with a local business bureau, such as the Better Business Bureau in the US and Canada. Make certain there are

"Clients want to rely on their freelance designer. We must be careful with this: although they can rely on us, it does not mean we are available 24/7."
Cinthy Revilla, Diseñadora Gráfica, Lima, Peru

1

1 "Glow is the right kind of client because they have a clear idea of what their brand is, and what they want to say. But they also realize why they hired me," says designer Tracie Haner Valentino. "They aren't afraid to give feedback—positive or negative—but still respect my experience and opinion. Plus, they feed me—rather well, I might add."
Photo: Karen Heerlein; copy: Bill Bonato and Tracie Valentino

2 Freelancer Tracie Valentino won an award from the Conneticut Art Directors Club for this stationery design for a women's clothing store.

no claims, liens, or complaints against the client. Also read the business section of your local newspaper to stay up to date with mergers and closures.

In any meeting situation, keep your wits about you. Stay calm and objective. For instance, if discord is arising between members of the client organization, don't try to play peacemaker. Instead, focus on the project at hand, and if that is impossible, excuse yourself for the time being. Or, if a client phones you in a distinctly nasty mood, listen carefully and try to discern the true source of his annoyance. Is it something to do with the project or because his car was just towed away?

Remember, too, that while this may be the only project you are working on, the client may have dozens of assignments, obligations, and meetings he is trying to juggle. To get his proper attention, make and keep strictly scheduled

appointments, in person or on the phone. Set up a regular time every day for a phone or email update, perhaps in the morning, before the day gets too busy.

The freelance designer will frequently have to play junior psychologist. Did a client say "no" to a design in a meeting because his boss was standing there or because he truly didn't like the work? If no response is forthcoming by email or phone, is the client just too busy to respond or is there a general lack of excitement for the solution? Your best solution is to simply ask—perhaps privately or at a later time. Often, fears are ungrounded.

When things really do get tangled, try to stay faithful to the person who brought you into the project in the first place. For instance, if proofs come back with comments from lots of different people, work with the main contact to decide which items to address. Also try to arm your in-house champion with answers to design questions colleagues may present: "Why can't we fill up this white space?" is a question you can answer once to your advocate, instead of over and over in various meetings or rounds of comps. Knowing the answer can help that person justify his choice in you and, ultimately, in any final design solution.

How to fire a client

When a client is simply a poor fit, it's in everyone's best interest to make the break. This need not be an acrimonious event; instead, keep it calm and professional. You may never want to work with that client again, but do try to leave on good terms. Remember that he or she can poison the water for you by giving a poor referral to people you might want to work with in the future.

Consider the following factors to protect your good name:

- If you are in the midst of a project and think you can carry it to completion, do so. But do not accept any future projects from that client.

- If you are in the midst of a project and do not think you can carry it through to completion, give them—and yourself—a graceful way out by providing a list of other designers who might be able to help them.

- If you are in the throes of a project that you cannot complete, offer a two-week notice period, or more.

- Offer to take the project to a logical stage of completion—when layout is finished, for instance—and ask the client to bring in someone else to take over after that.

- If you're really desperate to escape and are willing to take a cut in pay, offer a discounted price for your work in order to extricate yourself. The loss of money is usually compensated by the boost in mental health.

"I had the opportunity to work onsite, and I would never do it again. You are the odd man out. The supervisor hung over my shoulder and nickel-and-dimed a tiny ad for eight hours. I could have had it done in two hours."

Freelance designer working in Indiana, US

"If you feel uncertain about a potential job, don't take it."

Damang Chassianda, Freelance designer, Indonesia

2

 The School of Life is a new cultural enterprise based in central London offering intelligent instruction on how to lead a fulfilled life. Freelancers Susanna Edwards and Joseph Harries were brought in as the designers-of-record as well as advisors. "[We] feel an affinity with and understand the concept," Edwards says.

Effective Partnering

How to be a Good Partner

"The sales brochures should be ready for your reps on Thursday, and the website will open Friday night," Michael told the client sitting across the table from him. It was a sunny Tuesday morning. "Everything is right on schedule."

The client nodded, leaning back in his chair and clasping his hands behind his head. "Yes, but there's a new wrinkle: the sales director now wants 100 folders printed with the new four-color logo on Thursday as well. Can you do that?"

Michael made a quick mental calculation. Of course, it could be done, but such a short run in just two days would cost his client a fortune. But he did have a connection with that digital printer downtown...

"How about four-color stickers on a prefab folder?" Michael asked.

"Sold!" the client smiled, visibly relieved.

A good partnership is usually the result of the same combination of things that makes a good friendship or marriage, says freelance designer Eleni Swengler of Baltimore, US: honest and open communication, respect, and trust.

"It also means proving to the client that you understand their needs and can solve their communication problems," she adds.

Freelancer Chris O'Connell from New York City says that strong partnership also involves the ability to compromise, establishing proper boundaries, and, "of course, learning the hard way."

"Within these skills," he says, "the most useful early on in any project is communication, and then, during the project, knowing when communication gives way to compromise. Let's face it, no matter what your design sense or technological know-how says, the client wants what the client wants. If you can't tactfully convince them that a color, font, or interface is in

poor judgment, there are times you have to put your ego aside and just give them what they want."

There are times, of course, when clients don't know what they want. This is especially true with start-ups or other groups new to design. So one of the best ways to partner with your clients is to thoroughly explore their needs—not just their wants. A savvy freelancer may be able to suggest a new (and more appropriate) medium or approach and land himself a new assignment in the process. Learn everything you can about the client's business so that you can make intelligent, innovative suggestions.

If a client persists in going toward what you see as a bad decision, sometimes the word "no" can be the right answer—at least, it is the answer a true partner would give.

"Explain why you think it is a bad idea. The reaction to the 'no' will tell you a lot about how much your client values your services and whether or not they consider you an asset," explains designer Michael

1

Wisniach of 3rd Cherry Designs, Texas, US. "Ideally, you want to partner with clients who believe you are an asset that can help build their company."

Wisniach points out that when a client seems to be making a poor decision, sometimes he is simply trying to play a bigger part in the design process. If this is the case, give the client other ways to have more of a vote—offer more design options or simply contact them more often than you would other clients. "You may even intentionally misspell a word now and then so they can 'find' it. That sounds petty, I know, but it can be effective,"

Wisniach says. "Or, it can show that you aren't running a spell-check. So be careful."

Explain things clearly. Remember that no one wants to appear or feel ignorant, including clients. While someone across the table may nod and appear to understand what you say, he may well have no idea what you are talking about. Design lingo and techno-talk abounds in the creative world, so take the time to explain it to the client, and whenever possible, avoid jargon.

The reverse also holds true. When a client lapses into jargon common in his world, and you don't understand it, say so as soon as possible. A client will usually see questions as a sign of your interest in his business, not as ignorance or ineptitude. If you want a client to be loyal to

"How do you succeed as a successful freelancer? It's the Golden Rule. Treat others as you want to be treated. It's really that simple."

Amy McAdams, Freelance designer, Indianapolis, US

you, it stands to reason that you should be loyal to them. This means not working with their competitors. Look out for their best interests when it comes to price and other measurables. Don't badmouth the client, especially in blogs or other very small worlds. Telling tales—even if they are perfectly true—has a way of biting one in the behind.

Be respectful of the client's resources. Don't waste their time by being late for meetings or making unnecessary calls. Be prepared for meetings. If there is a question mark over the hours spent on a project, always bill in favor of the client. Look at every aspect of every project: if design A costs more to mail than design B, point this out. If a website would serve the company better than yet another brochure, say so.

It's also possible to bring even more resources to a client, explains Jose Nieto, a freelancer from Massachusetts, US. In fact, you can deliver an entire team. "I have established relationships with people who can do it all—a copywriter, web developer, a printer. I can take all of these troubles from the client's desk and provide comfort for him," he says. "People feel overwhelmed a lot of the time. If you have a can-do attitude and show them that you can solve their problems, maybe while delighting them and staying on budget and on the timeline, you are their perfect partner."

If you know a client's line of business well, you can get involved with them in ways other designers can't or won't, notes designer Michael Wisniach. "Ask to look at internal forms, packaging, shipping labels, and internal communications so you can look for more opportunities to shape the client's brand, needs, and ultimately, build repeatable business."

Be available, even when the schedule is crazy. This may mean simply picking up the phone when it rings or just responding promptly to texts or emails. It can mean having an "out of office" message on your email or phone if you are out of town or just away for a few hours, so the client doesn't think you simply aren't responding. It may also mean kindly turning down work if the schedule doesn't permit (but also offering the name of another designer). The key is to provide the client with the sense that he is indeed working with a real partner and is definitely not alone in the design process.

Another simple partnering gesture is to follow up after a project is complete. Ask how implementation of the design is going. Just investing a few minutes to check in with a client can make him feel special and yield additional projects down the road.

1 Designer Jani Whitesides needed the client's help to communicate the message and energy of the client's one-woman keynote performance. "She really committed to the process, and our collaborative relationship made it a successful piece," Whitesides says.

Metode Penelitian Komunikasi

etnografi

KOMUNIKASI

Suatu Pengantar dan Contoh Penelitiannya

Prof. Dr. Engkus Kuswarno, M.S.

widya PADJADJARAN

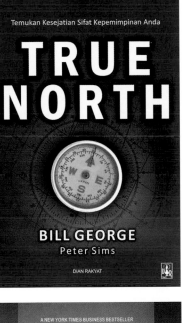

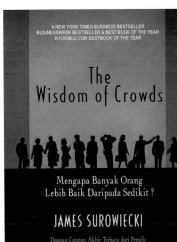

can develop from existing
ones, as happened for
Damang Chassianda
Sarumpaet. An existing
partner—an instructor
from college—referred
him to Dian Rakyat, one
of the oldest and most
established publishing
houses in Indonesia.
The publisher gave him
a trial job, and it was a
success. That led to many
additional projects, some
of which are shown here.

2

1 MedFit Partners is what freelancer Jennifer Wambach calls a perfect client: it allows almost total creative freedom, doesn't make a lot of changes, gives generous deadlines, and pays on time. As a result, she has been working with the client since 2005, including on this design for a spa brochure.
Art direction: Robin Schuette

How can you get good feedback from your clients?

Check in regularly. Ivancka Kroell of Durban, South Africa, updates her clients weekly on her progress and requests immediate feedback on whether or not she is on the right track.

Encourage the client to give an honest appraisal of your work. Create an atmosphere in which they feel comfortable speaking frankly. Sometimes clients may not want to hurt your feelings, but if the work is not serving their needs and is ultimately unsuccessful, their business is not served well, and you may lose a client—an unhappy ending for everyone.

"I tell my clients that it's OK not to like something because design is often subjective," notes Eleni Swengler. "But if they don't like it, I ask them to communicate why. If they can verbalize what's bothering them, that enables me to find a better solution."

Sometimes feedback is very hurtful, however. This can be one of the most difficult hurdles to overcome—but don't take unpleasant feedback personally. Get over the sting and try to really listen to what that person is saying (however gracelessly they may be saying it). If the other person is simply being insensitive, don't let his poison infect your work or energy.

What is the formula that turns a one-time client into a repeat customer?

To win a repeat customer, a freelancer must balance both sides of an equation: heart and wallet. If a client loves you but can't afford your services, you've lost them just the same as if they hated your work. Conversely—and probably even worse—if you're affordable but not liked, it's the door for you.

There is no one formula that balances this equation for every client. One may love the holiday gifts you send, while another might never even mention having received it. One may be annoyed when you dutifully check in with project progress reports while another may expect two or three calls a day. How can you win?

The repeat customer grows from a bespoke relationship in which the client feels he is not only getting good service and design, but also that you genuinely care about his organization's welfare. It is a relationship that you can create and nurture. The ways in which you can

2 Created for a delivery van for a concept store in Dubai called Five Green, the detail in these graphics is emblematic of the work of London-based designer Adam Hayes. He worked closely with the store's owner to make sure the van reflected the vibe of the store.

WHAT DOES YOUR CLIENT WANT?

New York City-based designer Chris O'Connell has an interesting approach to learning more about what exactly a client wants.

"Reaching into the pop-psychology pocket in my bag of tricks, I often try to get the client to mentally visualize their end product before I even start working. I'm not afraid to be corny and tell them to close their eyes and take a deep breath. I tell them to imagine it is a week or two past deadline and they are looking right at the end product and people are complimenting them on it and such.

"'What do you see?' I'll ask as I press for whatever details I can get, taking as many notes as possible. From there, it's just a matter of using their keywords to free the statue from the rock, if you will. With this approach, it is usually hard to go too far off course. When revision is needed, the client feels more connected to the end product and is often very clear and emphatic about what is needed at each stage."

existing client, hears that the same client has hired a different freelancer for an upcoming job. It's easy to feel hurt or even "fired" in such a situation. Truth is, though, the client simply may have needed a different set of design skills for the upcoming job. It does not mean that the client now hates your work or will never call you again. The relationship is still intact, and the freelancer should continue to court the client in the usual way.

Be sincere, says Pau Ricart Masip, a Spanish freelancer working in Ecuador. "If you don't know how to do something, just say it. Because if you try to deceive your clients, they will never call you again. I say 'no' sometimes, and it's true that I lose some clients, but I have happy ones, too," he says.

demonstrate that caring are many and varied; there is no "one size fits all" approach.

Realize, too, that a single client's needs change over time, even from project to project—and that's absolutely no reflection on your abilities. One common freelancing scenario is when a designer, basking in the glow of a just-completed project with a new or

One final consideration in developing repeat clients: a client may offer plenty of work, be high-profile, and have a great budget, but do you really and truly want to work with them again? Perhaps the work is deadly dull, or the schedule too restrictive. It may be hard to walk away from such a gig, but remember a problematic or troublesome client poisons the creative well over time. Remember that you are the boss of you; you can give yourself permission to walk away.

"Ask, ask, ask—and not just about the work to be done, but about the entire process. Your client is pure gold. Even better—he is pure oxygen."

Christian Steagall-Condé, Freelance designer, Londrina, Brazil

1 Peruvian designer Cinthy Pilar Revilla Llanos' client was visiting for a very short period of time from Chile, which only gave her a week to create a completely new identity and stationery system for the client's family gynecological office. The project included this folder, a complete upgrade from the white folder printed with black letters the office had previously been using. The client was so pleased, she has remained with Revilla Llano, despite the long-distance relationship, and was in fact the first person to call the designer after Peru suffered a terrible earthquake in 2007.

1 Big projects require big partnerships between designer and client. Freelance designer Janice Davis from Brooklyn, US, created this entrance to the children's area in the Bayshore-Brightwaters Library. Davis says that the library and librarians were great partners, as was Chris Howard, the construction contractor.

What to do when things go wrong

Sometimes, regardless of a designer's best efforts, there is a schedule or budget blowout. Perhaps expectations aren't met, or maybe one of the parties involved has dropped the ball. In such cases, having all contractual paperwork signed and in place will be a lifesaver. Just knowing who is responsible for what—in writing—can be an objective roadmap to solving problematic situations before emotions take over. See Chapter 4 for more information on how to properly protect your business—and your sanity.

For less serious issues, speak honestly with the client as soon as possible. Keep a cool head: in some cases, it may make the difference between losing a client and gaining a lawsuit.

If you were in the wrong, admit it to the client and apologize. Tell them that you value them as a client and ask what you can do to rectify the situation. Perhaps you can offer a discount or offer additional services at no cost. Even if you are dismissed from the job, your reputation as a decent person and partner can be preserved.

If the client was in the wrong, there's no need to grind it in. Try to offer a compassionate solution, but keep the original contract close at hand and stick to it. Don't let your empathy get in the way of business sense.

Remember that at some point in your career, something is certain to go wrong. That doesn't mean that you are a bad designer, or that the client relationship is instantly ruined. You may never work with the client again, but try to leave the situation so that you both have your dignity. Your reputation is hugely valuable, and the world is very small indeed.

1

"I always take a client on the same level as a friend in business. We are equal. They have the money, and I have something they need."
Damang Chassianda, Freelance designer, Indonesia

1&**2** Creating designs for snowboards is great work; having a friend as a client is even better. Craig Hansen is allowed total creative freedom from client Sined for his pro bono work, and is also rewarded with a few sample boards and free lodging and lift tickets when he visits the client in Colorado. "Seeing my designs flying through the air in magazine ads or online is just awesome," he says. "I was a professional snowboarder myself years ago and would have killed to have been allowed to design my own graphics. It is wonderful and fulfilling to finally get that chance."

2

Managing Workflow

How to Organize Your Work

The best thing about working so late at night, Sophia thought, was that the phone was extremely unlikely to ring, delivering more requests or problems. Now, she could just work. Now, she could concentrate.

The catalog was on schedule—or would be, if she worked until 1 or 2 a.m. every night. This was week two of the project, and the schedule dictated that everything had to be at the printer by the end of week four.

Sophia had just finished page 33 when an email from the client popped into her Inbox. "Substitute the attached copy on pages 12–24," it read. Sophia suddenly realized how much her back hurt. She had had enough for tonight, but knew she would not sleep well, knowing that all of those pages had to be

reworked in the morning. Why couldn't things go more smoothly, just for once?

Many designers work better with a little pressure; others like a lot. There's nothing like an imminent deadline to inspire action.

But for longevity in the business, freelancers have to find ways to protect their sanity from the clock. A day, a week, or even a month of rush can be dealt with. But making chaos a way of life is a certain path to creative, emotional, and/or physical burnout.

Be aware that workflow problems are not just caused by clients and other outside influences. Often, they are caused by the designer him- or herself. So what can you do to keep workflow manageable?

Internal controls
Establish a routine
One of the main reasons why creatives go into freelancing is to regain control of their lives—that is, to determine their own daily schedules. Ironically, that heartfelt wish is sometimes not honored; the freelancer simply does not make the effort to establish a schedule.

It's likely that it is the dreaded word "routine" that turns some people off. Routines are predictable; routines are boring. But routines are also the best possible protection from stressed-out days, all-nighters, and no social life.

"The more I think of myself as a company [with regular hours], the easier it gets to deal with the clock. It doesn't need to be as painful as it sounds. Create a routine that works for you," advises Ed Peixoto, a Brazilian freelancer now based in Oregon, US. "For example, wake up early, hit the shower, eat breakfast, answer emails, make phone calls, work for a couple of hours, have a quick bite and a 45-minute workout, hit the shower again, work for a few more hours, and then enjoy the rest of your day."

Honor your rituals
Rituals border on routine, but have more to do with the common order of your nonworking life. Rituals aren't usually very exciting, but somehow, they help one's mental health. Consider the day of Savyra Meyer, a freelancer in Western Cape, South Africa, who works out of her home.

"On getting up, I make my bed before even leaving my bedroom. Then I perform my ablutions, having bathed the night before to relax those shoulders. After that, it's on with the makeup and clothes, after which the coffee and fruit salad.

1 The Indieana Handicraft Exchange crafting event needed a logo, but had little time and a relatively small budget. The organizers' only request was for the designer to incorporate the concept of Indiana, which Amy McAdams achieved by subtly incorporating the outline of the state into the logo's wrist. The project was completed in just 48 hours.

1

"Dishes are washed, the house is picked up a bit to create a feeling of harmony and peace. Whatever remains is left for lunch- or teatime," she says. The remainder of the day is compartmentalized into predictable work, break, and eating times. "It's important to let go of the trivial and get to your work. People who are employed [in offices] do it all the time, every day."

However, Meyer does resist being completely controlled by the clock. "To take advantage of the 'free' in 'freelance' makes you feel like a million dollars, so to stop by a coffee or book shop after dropping off work at a client's office, then to go select three books with a cappuccino, then read them later in the bath... I also feel so fortunate when I lie in bed in the morning and listen to all those commuters zooming by on the streets below," she says.

Have a backup plan

When "the idea" doesn't come easily, remember the techniques that have helped to shake loose ideas in the past. Maybe visiting a gallery or reading the newspaper or running helps. Don't sit there and stew; get up and do something else—but keep it focused.

Prioritize

Know what is most urgent and what can wait another day. Don't let online solitaire or paying the utility bill interfere with normal work hours.

Prioritizing also extends into communication with printers and other contractors—let them know what needs attention first.

Screen your calls. It may feel awkward to "hide" from friends or family, but all those minutes spent chatting not only eat your schedule alive, they also break the concentration.

Focus

Prioritizing leads to focus. Develop exterior mechanisms that help you to focus, such as a door that shuts.

"Owing to circadian rhythms, most people are more alert early in the morning and before lunch. Thereafter, it's siesta time. I eat, take a 20-minute nap, and that does the trick. I also take another 20–30 minute break to walk my dog. It's a great way to regroup and get a fresh look at your work, as well as stretching the body from that deadly seated position."

Nanette Ferreri, Freelance designer, New Jersey, US

Turn off the music or turn it way up. Ask for the cooperation of the people with whom you live. Unplug the internet and turn off the phones.

You can also develop internal focusing mechanisms. Concentrate on the ultimate goal. The task in hand is to finish the job, but client satisfaction and a continued relationship is the ultimate goal.

Many creatives also use the "carrot and stick" approach, although sometimes they employ it in reverse. When lack of focus is allowed to become a way of life, the punishment-stick of little sleep, horrible nutrition, and no free time is applied. But life can be so much more pleasurable if you create a tangible reward-carrot that is awarded once the work is done. Can you bribe yourself? Certainly—call it an incentive, if you wish, just like corporations do. The possibilities are endless and range from imagining the satisfaction that will be felt once the job is successfully completed to taking a special vacation or making a special purchase. After all, deciding to be a freelancer is rooted in the desire to become your own boss. You might as well be an appreciative, munificent one.

Set allotments

Although no two jobs are ever the same, it can make sense to set time quotas for certain jobs. For instance, a designer might decide that three days is a reasonable amount of time in which to design a logo for a small business. That does not mean that he can only spend three days on every small-business logo project, but it provides a preset window that is useful in scheduling.

2 On a Wednesday afternoon, freelance designer Brooke Goans received an assignment to create a new logo for an internal software program. On Friday morning, she presented four concepts to the client. One was approved that same afternoon—and Brooke was asked to create two posters by Monday morning.

"If you have a deadline that demands a few extra hours, try to spread them out over the week so that you're not spending late nights in front of your machine, as this will definitely dampen your enthusiasm and affect the quality of your work."
Ivancka Kroell. Freelance designer. Durban. South Africa

solutions at your desktop
inforward

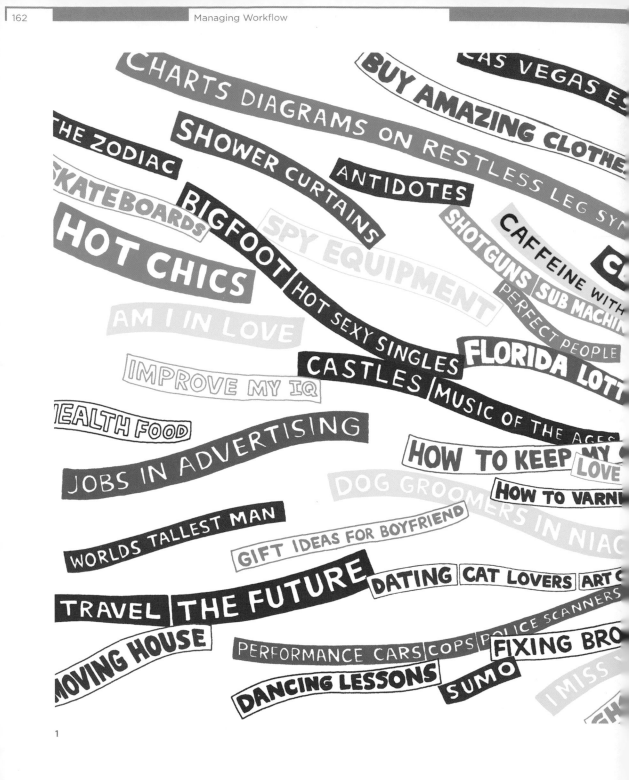

1 London-based freelancer Adam Hayes created this double-page spread for the *G2* section of *The Guardian* newspaper in just a day and a half. "This was achieved by dropping everything else and showing every stage of the work to the art director to make sure it was progressing in the right direction," he says.

They know all about you

Every time you use an internet search engine, your inquiry is stored in a huge database. Would you like such personal information to become public knowledge? Yet for thousands of AOL customers, that nightmare has just become a reality. **Andrew Brown** reports on an incident that has exposed how much we divulge to Google & co

1 Adam Hayes only had one day to create this illustration of an area in Madrid for the Travel section of *The Guardian* newspaper. It was particularly tricky, he says, as everything had to be geographically accurate, and there were to be 24 further illustrations in the series. He had to create a style that would be versatile enough for future, as-yet-unknown articles.

The never-ending to-do list

It's ironic that a simple sheet of paper can weigh so heavily on one's psyche. Instead of creating a to-do list for the entire universe of your life, first cleanse the list of anything that is not concerned with work. Then take the remaining tasks and assign them to specific days or hours. Focus on the week at hand. If there's overflow, move some tasks into the following week.

Any jobs that are especially large and unwieldy—"finish my master's degree," for example—may need to be broken down into small parts— "check class catalog online on Tuesday," for instance.

Get organized and stay that way

When things are hectic, it's tough to keep up with filing, billing, or even dusting. If organization is not your strong suit, reward yourself with a day to reorder and declutter the office. Clean it thoroughly and set up a system that works for you. Then, once a week—maybe on a Friday afternoon as the kickoff to the weekend—spend a few hours catching up. Make that time sacrosanct. Even better, make it enjoyable: listen to a CD or have a glass of wine. Hang new art or do other decorating that you've been planning so that your workspace improves week after week.

If you simply do not have the time or aptitude to get organized, hire someone to do it for you. Professional organizers are not hard to find, and for a reasonable fee they can make day-to-day life in the office much less stressful.

Get ahead of the game

Anything a designer can do to get a few steps ahead yields free time later. Even better, it opens up time for the unexpected, like a friend's invitation to lunch or a nap when you really need it.

But this means not spending hours pondering whether red or blue is better or losing yourself in a million other details that really aren't all that important. Consider whether each time-zapping decision will really be worth it later on.

It's no surprise to designers that the creative process almost always takes longer than anticipated. So to compensate for that inevitable lost time, spend less time on detail and more on planning. Consider having someone else draw up your plans, if planning is the greatest priority.

Don't procrastinate

That's often more easily said than done. How is it done? "Don't waste time on crap," says Savyra Meyer. What's crap? Meandering around on the internet when there's real research to be done, she says, or watching TV just because everyone else is lounging.

"The clock is the chief we do not have as freelancers. But sometimes designers feel they are racing the clock and it often plays out badly when we are checking details. The stress causes us to lose our good humor."
Adrian Abdala, Freelance designer, Argentina

"You could be polishing the furniture because it smells so nice or deciding today is the day the family photos must go into albums because you could die someday and then no one will know where it all goes. Or, a magazine arrives in the post, and now it's teatime, and oops—that time is gone forever. It's not constructive time, as is a long walk on the beach, or time spent looking at the stars, or listening to music, or spending time with your partner, friends, and family. It's useless, not even very pleasurably spent time," she points out.

One can decide to be alert to procrastination and cut it short. Forego a "good time" for much better-quality time.

"I believe that particular notion of 'sanity' or 'insanity' is guilt-driven nonsense. Do all you can do, and whatever happens is what happens. No matter what numbers appear on the clock, whining, blaming, or playing 'what if' serves nothing. Either you do a good job and nail the deadline, or you find something to learn from the situation."
Chris O'Connell, Freelance designer, Massachusetts, US

❶ After the rush of everyday projects, it's good to stretch the creative muscles. The illustration shown here provided a beneficial change of pace for Radim Malinic of Brand Nu in Southampton, UK. "Zemog El Gallo Bueno" was an experiment with color and textures that has now become a stepping stone in his portfolio.

Beware of the internet

"Creative people are naturally oriented to curiosity and like to attain new knowledge or points of view," says Christian Steagall-Condé, a freelance designer from Londrina, Brazil. "Before you go online to do research, set a time limit and obey it," he adds.

Email can also be a horrible drain on focus. Pick just a few times in the day to roll through it—maybe first thing in the morning and then again in the late afternoon—and don't worry about it the rest of the time. And turn off instant messaging while you're at work, as well as message notification on email and phones.

Don't overdo it

When you've done what you set out to do for the day, stop. When you have completed the project to the client's satisfaction, stop. Your free time is essential for continued creative health.

Keep on marketing

When times are hectic, self-promotion often falls to the bottom, and then off, the to-do list. But consistent marketing ensures a consistent flow of work. When the schedule is slow, take advantage of the downtime to prepare self-promos that can be sent out quickly during busy times.

External influences

There are numerous external factors that can sabotage even the most organized freelancer's schedule. Read the following list and be aware of the pitfalls.

Distant clients

Working with clients in other time zones can push your workday earlier or later. If that happens, try to maintain the same number of hours you would normally work, instead of tacking time onto the front or back of your day. Return to your regular schedule as soon as it is practical.

"Emergency" projects

Another schedule-killer is the client who thinks that freelancers are available all hours of the day or night, or all weekend, or on a holiday. There's a straightforward solution to this dilemma: a simple "no" will usually suffice. However, one freelance designer has a more graceful, and potentially more lucrative, answer to the problem. "Lately, I have started to mention that I charge a higher fee if I have to work over the weekend. This has been fairly successful in weeding out those jobs that aren't really an emergency," she says. "It's amazing sometimes how those jobs that have to get done by tomorrow can suddenly wait until next week."

"Sometimes the most difficult part of the day is to click 'Shut Down....' Creativity is like a way of life, but you can get inspired by what is all around you, not just in front of you, in the computer."

Alexandre Soubrier, Freelance designer, Paris, France

1

Know where you're going

Never, ever begin a project without a fully detailed brief and a complete understanding of the project's ultimate goal. A client who is unsure or badly prepared breeds a schedule destined to fail. Think of the project like a trip: you have to know where you are going before you can plan how to get there.

Meeting hell

Meetings are a necessary evil, and it is within the freelancer's power to take control and prevent time-wasting. First, determine with the client a set time and day, every week, when a meeting can occur. That way, the time is already blocked out on the schedule. Second, meet in the client's office so that you can leave promptly when business is done. Otherwise, you may end up with a client who is enjoying being away from his office and won't leave your space.

If meetings start spiraling out of control, let the client know that you are charging for your time. Things are likely to get more efficient very quickly.

Family and friends

It's all too common to have people dropping by just because you work at home or in a small office by yourself. Or, people ask for your time during the day—to run errands, to babysit, to have lunch, and so on. They may mean well, but unless you firmly put an end to it, your schedule will be adversely affected and bad feelings will erupt.

Mundane duties

For duties that are boring or repetitive—backing up your files, for instance, or fetching mail from the post office—look for ways to automate them or get someone else to do the job. Hiring someone to clean your office is not only time-efficient, it's a huge mood-booster (and it's a business expense that is tax-deductible). Maybe it costs a little extra for the overnight delivery guy to pick up at your place, but consider how much it costs for you to run down to their office every time you need to ship.

Everyday life

It can be frustrating to have to stop work every day at 3 p.m. to pick up the kids from school. Maybe an upstairs neighbor cranks the tunes every morning around 10 a.m. Since there's not much you can do to change the pace of everyday life, embrace these interruptions instead. Use the trip to school to also get a coffee or take a brisk walk. When the music starts, take a break from the desk. Find a way to welcome the interruption rather than fret about it.

TIME-MANAGEMENT TOOLS FOR FREELANCERS

As technology has proliferated, so have time-management tools for small businesses and designers. There are literally hundreds of time- and project-management applications available on the internet; the ones listed here were mentioned specifically by designers interviewed for this book.

Some of these tools only track time as it applies to billing, but many have other excellent features as well. Make sure that what you choose can be synchronized with the technology you are already using: that is, your computer platform, PDA, phone, or any other device.

Commercial software

Creative Manager Pro (www.creativemanagerpro.com):
  Ad agency project-management software
Basecamp (www.basecamphq.com): Web-based project-management service
JobCapture (www.captureworks.com): Project-management software
Harvest (getharvest.com): Online time-tracking software
Freshbooks (www.freshbooks.com): Online time-tracking and invoicing software
Tempo (keeptempo.com): Online time-tracking software
yaTimer (www.nbdtech.com/yaTimer): Time-management software
AcuInvoice (www.acuinvoice.com): Online invoicing and estimation software
Copper (copperproject.com): Project-management software
Easy Time Tracking (www.easytimetracking.net/index.asp):
  Time-management and customer billing software
FourteenDayz (www.14dayz.com): Online time-tracking software
Bento 2 (www.FileMaker.com/Bento): Personal organizational software
PunchyTime (www.punchytime.com): Online time-management software
@Task (www.attask.com): Project and portfolio management software

Freeware

Remember the Milk (www.rememberthemilk.com): Online task-management software
Ta-da Lists (www.tadalist.com): Online to-do list service

Other time-management resources

There are many other time-saving resources available online. Freebies that can be modified or customized such as templates, design tools, Photoshop actions, Illustrator brushes, and so on, can be very useful.

"Places like DeviantArt.com offer some great tools and resources for Photoshop and Illustrator," says Theraisa Fleig, a freelance designer from Ontario, Canada. "Download.com offers some great programs and tools for designers. Likewise, just Googling things like 'free templates' or 'free Photoshop actions' can lead you to unlimited sources of tools and information that can help get the project done faster."

Managing subcontractors

There may be times when a freelancer lacks sufficient time or knowledge to complete an entire project, and in these cases bringing in another designer to help with layout or a programmer to help pull a website together can make perfect sense. But bringing in subcontractors can be a mixed blessing.

One freelancer recalls the year in which she earned far more than she ever had before, managing a set of

1

publications for a very large client. To get the work done, she had to hire three additional designers, all friends with whom she had worked in the past.

"At first, it was a lot of fun," says the designer, "and the money was terrific. But as a sole proprietor, I wasn't really set up to be that kind of a manager or to deal with things like filing tax forms on their behalf. All I did was work!"

Even the perks the position afforded were soon overshadowed by the job. She planned a vacation for her family with the extra cash, but found herself stopping at fast-food joints again and again to spread out layouts on greasy tables and consult with her subcontactors via the cellphone.

"It just wasn't worth it. I eventually resigned the account, and my income dropped by $50,000 in one year. It made me a bit queasy to do it, but I was a lot happier," she says.

"Billing clients is a good problem to have, but I don't get paid to do it, nor is it fun for me."

Eric Benoit, Freelance designer, Boston, US

2

3

1-**3** The Criminal Records store was moving and had very little time to inform its customers. Within 48 hours, designer Amy McAdams had designed and printed posters that resembled old grocery signs. They stood out perfectly among the rock posters that were already in the store's windows.

In order to land some larger accounts and more money, it is sometimes necessary to bring in additional help. (If you are working on any sort of non disclosure basis with a client, obtain their permission before bringing anyone else into the project.) But each additional person increases the size of your to-do list. The key is to balance the reward—satisfaction, money, and/or prestige—against what's necessary to get the job done.

"Managing subcontractors has to take less time than designing. If not, you can become a project manager," says French freelancer Alexandre Soubrier.

It's crucial to have complete confidence in anyone you bring into the project: it's your name on the client contract, and your reputation that is at stake. Make certain that subcontractors understand your expectations and follow up frequently to make sure everyone is on schedule and on budget.

Make sure subcontractors understand the project as well as you do. Get all of the details of the business and creative relationship on paper—in short, prepare everything a client might prepare for you, such as a contract, a brief, a timeline, and so on. Define the amount of decision-making power the subcontractor has to prevent misunderstandings later. Consult with an accountant or tax specialist on how to properly account for payments to any subcontractor.

Handling large or long-term projects

Large or long-term projects can feel a bit daunting for the freelancer, especially at first. If you consider such a project as a single, giant entity, it can quickly become overwhelming. But with the proper planning it's possible to make even the largest project manageable.

■ Break the project into pieces. Dividing the job into many smaller stages helps to make it seem more achievable. If you still feel overwhelmed, break the pieces into even smaller pieces. It might help to set a time limit for each piece—this not only keeps you on schedule, but also brings the light at the end of that particular tunnel into view.

Ask to be paid at the completion of each piece or at a regularly scheduled time—at the end of every week, for instance.

- Celebrate each piece. When you finish, say, the research portion of a project, balloons and streamers will not fall from the ceiling. But that doesn't mean you shouldn't celebrate. Reward yourself with a few hours off or a special meal with a friend. Some people derive a lot of satisfaction just from ticking off items on a list of duties or crossing off successfully completed days on a calendar. Even just telling a friend or family member who will respond with the appropriate, "Nicely done!" can feel great.

- Keep the schedule up to date. For the client, provide a copy of the job's schedule. If the designer or client pushes back deadlines, provide an updated schedule to help keep everyone calm and informed.

- Get help. Be aware of colleagues and other professionals to whom you might subcontract part of the work. Perhaps they can take

over less enjoyable parts of the job or tasks that normally challenge you.

- Don't let familiarity breed contempt. Long-term or large projects naturally result in more familiar relationships with clients. Sometimes that's good—trust is established and healthy partnerships form. But sometimes a client abuses that familiarity by asking for endless changes, for instance, or ignoring a schedule.

Massachusetts-based designer Chris O'Connell relates the story of a peer who was being treated badly by a long-term and prestigious client. But the friend endured it because business was slow and he wanted the gig for his portfolio. It's unhealthy, O'Connell says, to become so attached to a position or project that you feel trapped.

"You should not be afraid to be upfront or even slightly aggressive with a client in letting them know what you need from them in order to be effective," he says.

- Stay organized. No matter how busy the project becomes, keep up with filing, billing, paperwork, and all of those non-design tasks that most designers would like to ignore. Keep excellent records both during and after the project.

"I make a mind-map for myself and the client. Then we agree on progress payments. The job stages are treated as separate jobs."

Savyra Meyer, Freelance designer, Western Cape, South Africa

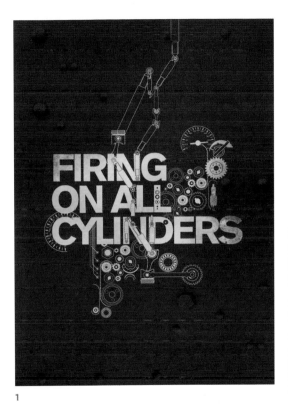

1

1 & **2** Radim Malinic of Brand Nu describes these projects as explorations in working with type. "Telling a story using a typographical message is pure joy [for me] and a nice change from normal illustration," he says.

2

Achieving a Work/Life Balance

How to Avoid Being a Work Addict

"Sometimes I think you're addicted to your work," Carita's husband said, leaning on the door to her office. He smiled and winked at her. "I'm heading to bed."

"I only have a few files left to do," Carita said, smiling back. But his words struck home. It was past midnight, and here she was again—working. But it didn't seem like work at all. In fact, if her eyes didn't get so tired, she thought she could work around the clock.

But was she addicted to her work? Is that what other people thought? She had always felt that design was her life, but had work become her life?

Is it possible to become addicted to one's work, to the point where work becomes preferable to any other activity? Sure. Anything that's pleasurable to human beings releases endorphins in the brain, and those endorphins make you feel good. People like to feel good, so they repeat those actions over and over, until the activity that spawns those feelings becomes an irresistible habit.

Design is (usually) a highly pleasurable activity. For designers, the exciting sense of exploration, rewarded by discovery and, ultimately, satisfaction, is the very definition of "fun." Endorphins abound, and the designer is rewarded by pleasurable feelings. Who wouldn't become addicted to that?

Many freelance creatives would readily admit to being addicted to what they do (or in the broader sense, to art and design). That's good news for clients. But for the freelance designer, who tends to be a very focused and hardworking person by nature anyway (you couldn't be in this business if you weren't), it can turn into tunnel vision over time. Without the light of the outside world shining in, a designer's creative health suffers.

No matter how busy you are as a freelancer, there are simple ways to inject space between you and your work.

Balancing work and life

The vast majority of designers, freelance or otherwise, usually work more than 40 hours per week; it's the nature of the beast. But there are some who work much more than that—50, 60, 70 hours, or more—and not just during a crunch week, but month after month. If you live alone and have absolutely no family or friends (or want to chase them away for good), and you choose that way of life freely, then it's obviously what you want.

But have you ever wondered if you're working too much? And how much is too much? The answer is simple: it's when work starts to negatively affect other parts of your life on a long-term or apparently endless basis. It's the normal human condition to have time to work and time to rest or play. But every human is different in his or her needs, so there's no preset, advisable number of hours. Perhaps the best gauge can be found in the eyes of the significant people in your life. If your partner, friends, family, or peers are concerned that you are working too much, then chances are you might be

---

"Fear of failure is also a factor which contributes to workaholism. The best thing I can do for myself is to focus on the moment and be as creative and productive as possible. It's the most anyone can do in a stressful situation. Fear and anxiety block creativity and productivity."

Rodney Davidson, Freelance designer, Alabama, US

1 Designer Søren Severin says he created this poster as a comical personal statement after many people commented that he did not use much color in his work. "I think it is important to think about what kind of designer you are and develop a personal sense of aesthetics. I have gotten a lot of positive feedback on the piece. I think it says a lot about me and my style," he says.

"But I have to make a living!" might be the freelancer's reply. Or, "I can't control when my clients need me!" But if every waking moment of your day is taken up with work, you might need to consider different clients, different kinds of design work, or some other alteration in your long-term plans in which the financial return on your investment of time is more favorable. It's not an alteration that can be made overnight, but at some point, the slow switch can start.

Even then, will work time ooze into private time? Certainly. Life, like work, is unpredictable. But when a designer works a 60-hour week, balance needs to be restored eventually. Remember that you are your own boss, and you can reward yourself sometimes.

"Sometimes my friends borrow me for a day, and we go for a tour through the wine lands or a day at the beach. But this often happens after a whole weekend was spent working," says Savyra Meyer of Western Cape, South Africa.

A hobby or outside interest is a great distraction from work. Many designers have hobbies that are related to their jobs, such as drawing, painting, or photography. But whatever pastime cleanses the palette of your mind, so to speak, is fine. It will increase the depth of your well of creativity, while you enjoy the time spent doing it.

"A hobby can turn into a journey that turns you into a better person," says Christian Steagall-Condé, a freelance designer from Brazil, "and chances are that you will become a better professional as a result."

Some freelancers give themselves permission to attend at least one distant design conference each year. Yes, it's a work-related trip, but such events almost always prove to be rejuvenating, whether you attend every session or decide to skip out for a few drinks. Gathering with one's peers is healthy medicine indeed.

"In order to maintain balance between my work and my private life, I don't work on weekends. I preserve those days for myself, to clear my mind and to have desire and ideas when I begin the next week."

Jimena Palecios, Freelance designer, Buenos Aires, Argentina

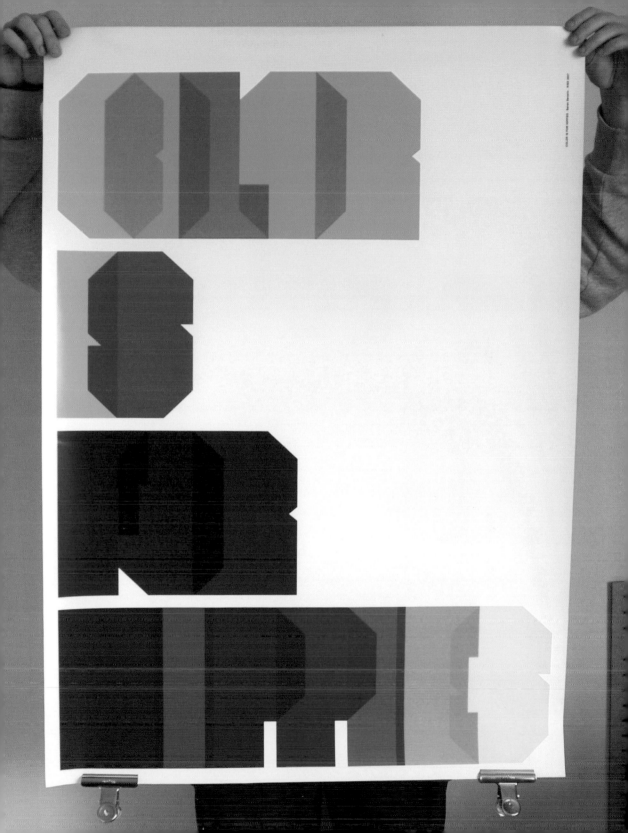

1

① Ceramics was a medium that designer Emily Alston had wanted to try for a while, and she finally got the chance when she was asked to participate in an exhibition. "Product design is something that many graphic designers are crossing over into," she says. "It was a bit of fun, but also another way of earning a wage."

Separating work and private space

How does one California-based designer separate her work and private space? "My husband stands in the doorway when I head for my computer in the evening," she says, not entirely joking. The more physical separation a freelancer can have between office space and home space, the better. That being said, plenty of successful, happy freelance designers have offices in their homes—some, in their bedrooms or one-room apartments (an idea no self-employment counselor would recommend, but sometimes it's unavoidable).

The physical space in which a freelancer works is often not something he or she can change. But there are other ways to introduce more separation between work and life:

- Even if you do work from your home, introduce some sort of physical barrier, such as a folding screen, behind which you can hide all of your work in off-hours.

"Keep work in a place where it won't distract you from everyday living, family, entertainment, or fun, and especially keep it away from your sleeping quarters," advises Theraisa Fleig, a freelancer from Ontario, Canada.

- Set up regular working hours—9 to 5, for instance—and do not violate them for any reason (other than emergency). Don't answer the phone when it rings after hours, and resist the temptation to check voice mail or email. It can wait until morning.

- If you are searching for a hobby, don't pick one that requires you to sit at the computer for hours and hours.

- Keep home and work office supplies separate. Otherwise, you'll be back in your office every time you need a piece of tape or a pair of scissors.

- Have a separate phone number for work, and if your office is in your home, forbid anyone else from answering it but you.

- If you have a home office, have client meetings off-site, at their offices or a coffee shop.

- There are clothes for work and clothes for home. Even freelancers with home offices should not wear pajamas to work, however tempting that may sound.

- Keep personal and work paperwork and finances separate.

Time off

The best way to get a vacation is to do exactly what people who work in offices do: schedule one. But that's the easy part; the hard part is actually following through and taking it. For a freelancer, the scary thing is that while you are on vacation you are not making money *and* you are still spending it (maybe even more than usual if on a trip away or if it's a gift-giving holiday).

The time that is scheduled as vacation must be made sacred. It's easier to do that if the time off is built around a religious or other holiday during which the world pretty much shuts down. But even

"I have come to realize that unless I balance the things that are important to me, I will not be able to truly enjoy any single one."

Maneesha Lee Jones, Freelance designer, Florida, US

if it's not, your time away should be scheduled and honored, by both you and your clients.

- Let clients know several months in advance that you will be away.

- Block that time out in a calendar and under no circumstances accept obligations for that period. Don't even plan to repaint the office or organize files.

- If you need external discipline to make sure you take the time away, put a nonrefundable deposit on a trip to a spa, hotel, or other vacation spot.

- Plan your time away carefully, just like you would a project, so that it will satisfy everything you were dreaming about when you were longing to get away.

2 Creating designs for tennis shoes has absolutely nothing to do with the rest of Cinthy Revilla's freelance work. But she enjoyed the experiments immensely.

2

1 Freelance designer Minakshi Jena gains inspiration from creating abstract digital art and photography. "Nature photography and the digital arts let me explore my creativity and help to rejuvenate me," she says.

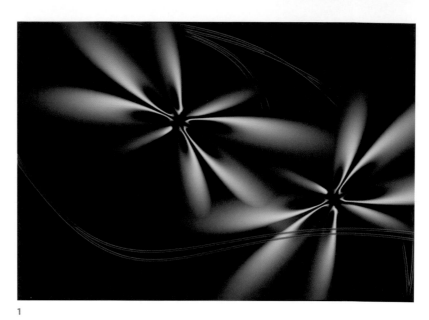

1

■ Save money for the trip so that finances aren't a reason to cancel.

■ Recruit your partner, friends, or family to help you get out on time.

To be realistic, not every waking moment of a freelancer's life is billable time. In fact, there's plenty of downtime. Christian Steagall-Condé points out that if a freelancer pushed all of his downtime together—that is, condensed it into one time block—it might total one or even two months. Instead of staying home and fretting about not having any work, he offers a palatable solution: "Vacation! Do not fight the numbers. Enjoy them," he says.

Here are some rules for your time off:

■ If you work out of your home, get away from the house. Go somewhere far away.

■ Do not take your computer or work with you.

■ Turn your phone off, and do not check email. Leave an away message on both that encourages callers or mailers not to leave a message, but rather to contact you when you return. Let clients know that you will not be retrieving messages.

■ Don't talk about work with anyone.

"It is not rocket science. If you pulled an all-nighter, take the next day off."

Eduardo Peixoto, a Brazilian freelancer now working in Oregon, US

VACATION: A CREATIVE NECESSITY

Janice Davis of Janice Davis Design, New York, US, has been a freelance designer for 26 years. She was a single mother who raised two children and was her family's sole support for many years. She has strong feelings about getting away from work, which she shares here.

"Do not skip vacation. In speaking with other freelancers, the most common excuse I hear for not taking vacations is the fear that their clients will find other designers to use in their absence and will continue to use those other designers even after they return. To these people, I'd make the following points:

- If you're truly good at what you do, are easy to work with, and are consistent in delivering a good product on time, you are not as easily replaceable as you may fear.

- If, as a designer and a creative individual, you do not take time to shut down the 'output' mode and go on 'intake' mode, your work will suffer and your ideas will run dry. You'll find that your projects all start to look alike, and that you are recycling the same old ideas again and again. It is not just pleasant or fun to get away to other environments, it is an absolute necessity when your career depends on your having to come up with new visions to communicate. Refreshing your creative juices cannot adequately happen in a long weekend. Personally, I don't even think it can happen in a week. By the time you wind down, it's time to gear up for reentry. The break should be at least two weeks, preferably three. Americans especially have an unfortunate expectation that a vacation is a (very) guilty pleasure, to be fit into a work schedule and gotten over with as quickly as possible. In some parts of Europe, a four, five, or even six-week vacation is the norm. Traveling to new places and having new experiences is part of life. This is not only emotionally healthy, it's creatively necessary.

- You owe it to your loved ones as well as yourself. A few weeks outside of your usual surroundings allows for a very different dynamic that refreshes and reaffirms relationships, be they parent–child, husband–wife, partner–partner, or friend–friend. Taking the time to devote to your family is not only wonderful in the space of those two weeks, but has the lasting benefit of resolidifying your relationships after you're home. It's that much easier to return to work knowing that your emotional life is that much more solid.

- It's much easier to effectively self-evaluate when you have a little distance (both physical distance and through the buffer of time). Switching gears, taking a new tack, expanding business horizons, and so on, are more difficult to think about clearly when you're in the thick of ongoing projects. With some time away, these decisions can be made with more clarity and objectivity."

"I sing in a choral group, which gives me great pleasure."

Rodney Davidson, Freelance designer, Alabama, US

Getting body and mind away

It's quite possible to take one's body away from the office. But the creative mind is always imagining, and the business mind is always thinking. It seems impossible to stop. This is perhaps one of the most difficult things for a freelance designer to do.

As you take your physical self away from the office, give your mind something else to think about. Getting away from the computer is a good start. Meander through bookshops or junk shops. Go to a gallery show. Buy a new book. Have long conversations with friends over drinks. In short, get out—it's that simple. Enjoy the experience and take the time to relish it afterward. Don't jump right back into work.

When you do get a chance to get away from work, whether it's for the evening or for several days, try to tie up any loose ends first. Also make a detailed to-do list for when you return. That way, you can confidently take your mind off work and know exactly where to start up when you return.

If you absolutely cannot get yourself—mind and body—away from work, ask a friend to help you. Pick someone who you think has a healthy outlook toward life, and explain your plight.

❶ "It's not always easy to find the time to create something off my own back, and when a spare moment does appear, it is often unexpected," says London–based designer and artist Adam Hayes. "I try to keep my personal and commercial work reflective of each other. I try to create something slightly different with my own work, and I consciously attempt to infiltrate those concepts into commercial projects. It's difficult to propose to a client a new style of work without being able to back it up with your own experiments."

❷ Freelance designer Craig Hansen paints regularly for inspiration. "I find myself incapable of going more than a week or so without it. Everything suffers, including my design work, if I don't do my art," he says.

2

Everyday recharging

If your vacation seems a long way off, or you really are too busy to take one, it's vital to take some regular time out to relax

- Join a local professional design organization and get involved with its social activities.

- Once in a while, use caller ID to screen calls from clients, even if it's only for an hour.

- Get involved in a new sport.

- Rearrange your office space, or paint, or just clean.

- Take a 20-minute power nap every day.

- Take a long bath or shower at the end of a long day.

"I do Latin and ballroom dancing three days a week and have started walking along the beach for two hours every second morning before I start work."

Savyra Meyer, Freelance designer, South Africa

Assessing Your Progress

How to Evaluate Your Success

If it hadn't been for her savings, these last few months would have been very difficult for Kate. When the new year had started, she was swamped. One job won a local advertising club award, and another client could not compliment her enough on her work. But now, nothing.

When she was busy, she had daydreamed about going back to school, or partnering with a local creative group, or taking time off. But now that free time had arrived, she was in an absolute quandary. Kate loved design. She loved freelancing. But this period of serious quiet had forced her to think hard: what did she want to do next?

In the rush of the everyday—and a successful freelance designer's life is certainly a rush day after day, in terms of both velocity and focus—self-examination is one of those chores that can be easily postponed. It's not necessarily time-consuming, but it can sometimes be unpleasant. And even if you do not find it hard to objectively scrutinize yourself, acting on those areas for improvement is an entirely different matter.

Evaluating your financial goals is usually quite simple; most freelancers know the status of their checking, savings, and credit accounts, for better or worse. But those other "accounts"—energy, satisfaction, knowledge, and skills—are less tangible.

How do you know how you are doing? An objective self-examination can be done with your short- and long-term business plans in hand (see Chapter 2). If you find that your business plan does not include such issues as continuing education, finding more desirable or profitable lines of work, or any other factors that indicate positive, forward growth, add them immediately. A successful businessperson is not only making money, but is happy as well. To that end, ongoing introspection is very helpful.

Self-evaluation

"Self-evaluations are very important so that we are able to notice advancements in our work and detect the failings," says freelancer Adrian Abdala. "They must be done in good conscience and without too much time passing by." A self-evaluation is not an obligation, he says, but it is necessary for any freelancer to achieve his or her goals.

A good self-evaluation reveals the stage you have reached in your progress toward particular goals. Once that is known, it's much easier to objectively identify whether your forward momentum is acceptable. If the progress rate is not adequate, you can make changes to rectify it. It's also wise to check that the goals that you have set for yourself are still "S.M.A.R.T."—a mnemonic that stands for Specific, Measurable, Attainable, Relevant, and Time-based. A periodic adjustment of goals is necessary as conditions change. Be realistic, not idealistic.

Build a block of time into your schedule once a month to perform a self-evaluation. Be ruthlessly objective and act on what you discover.

"Thousands of people want your way of life. But you need courage, focus, and persistence to be a freelance designer. Working this way for me is like having a tungsten heart with liquid steel flowing like blood."

Christian Steagall-Condé, Freelance designer, Brazil

1

① Freelance designer Brooke Goans was asked to redesign this publication. "I've never designed a publication, but they trusted it to me," she says.

A simple self-evaluation will help you isolate specific areas in which improvement or changes might be needed. Any question that can be answered with a "no" indicates an area for improvement.

1. Financial progress
a. I am able to pay my bills.
b. I am able to pay my bills and still save money/pay myself.
c. I am able to pay my bills, save money/pay myself, and also reinvest in my business.

2. Client connections
a. I have gained new clients.
b. I have kept all of my recent clients.
c. I have made contact with clients through marketing or other promotional effort in the past 30 days.

3. Resource network
a. I have access to the professional help that I need from peers and vendors in order to do business.
b. I am able to be an effective resource to others.

4. Technology
a. I have the computers, software, and other tools to do good work in an efficient manner.
b. I am moving into or toward the new technologies I would like to explore in the future.

5. Paperwork
a. I am up to date on billing and other financial issues.
b. I am up to date on filing and other office organization.

6. Pace of business
a. I am able to work at a pace with which I am comfortable most of the time.
b. I am working during the hours of the day or night that I prefer.

7. Ongoing education
a. I have availed myself of an educational opportunity at least once per week.
b. I have the education I need right now in order to stay competitive.

"Normally, a crisis brings [a self-evaluation] on. I sit down with my previous mind map of goals and see how far I've come, what has been achieved, and what still needs to be seen to. This involves aspects such as Body, Mind, Spirit, Emotions, Social, Financial, and Work."

Savyra Meyer, Freelance designer, Western Cape, South Africa

8. Personal relationships
a. I have healthy, satisfying
relationships with my clients.
b. I have healthy, satisfying
relationships with my family and
am able to spend adequate time
with them.
c. I have healthy, satisfying
relationships with my friends and
am able to spend adequate time
with them.

9. Community involvement
a. To the degree I desire, I am
involved with community/social
organizations or causes.
b. Local community/social
organizations are aware of my
business and the services I provide.

10. Future plans
a. I am moving toward specific
goals I have set for myself
b. I need to set goals (or additional
goals) for myself with an assigned
timeline for completion.
c. I have achieved a specific
goal recently and have rewarded
myself accordingly.

11. Personal reflection
a. I am proud of my work.
b. I feel my work makes the best
use of my talents.
c. I feel enthusiastic about the work
I do and want to continue with it.
d. To the degree I desire, I am able
to get away from work for rest
or recreation.

2

3

2 & **3** Both of these posters were created for plays, and together they represent a definite step forward in the career of designer Javier Escalante, who had not had many illustration commissions previously.

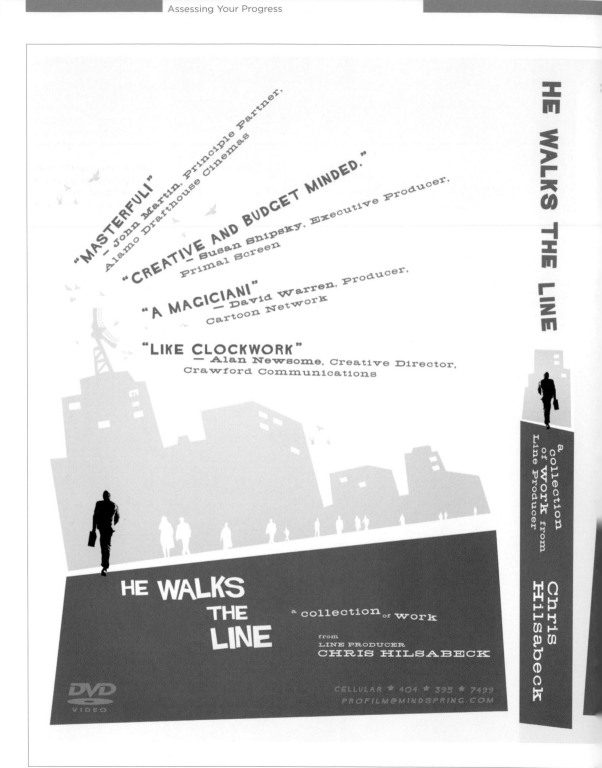

"MASTERFUL!"
— John Martin, Principle Partner,
Alamo Drafthouse Cinemas

"CREATIVE AND BUDGET MINDED."
— Susan Shipsky, Executive Producer,
Primal Screen

"A MAGICIAN!"
— David Warren, Producer,
Cartoon Network

"LIKE CLOCKWORK"
— Alan Newsome, Creative Director,
Crawford Communications

HE WALKS THE LINE
a collection of work

from
LINE PRODUCER
CHRIS HILSABECK

DVD
VIDEO

CELLULAR ★ 404 ★ 395 ★ 7499
PROFILM@MINDSPRING.COM

HE WALKS THE LINE

a collection of work from Line Producer

Chris Hilsabeck

...MANAGES. HE NEGOTIATES. HE LEADS...

HE WALKS THE LINE

ollection of work

from
LINE PRODUCER
CHRIS HILSABECK

1 When freelance designer James Christian of St. Louis, US, couldn't find an illustrator to create the Hitchcock look and feel he wanted for this design, he decided to give it a try himself and was pleased with the results. "Although I am not an illustrator by trade, this project gave me a lot of confidence in my ability to pull something off that I have never done before," he says.

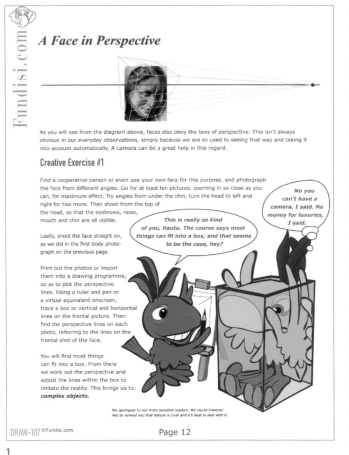

1

360-degree evaluations

In addition to completing a self-evaluation, you might also consider a 360-degree evaluation at least once per year. A 360-degree evaluation is when a group of peers provides feedback on your performance—sometimes anonymously, if that's more comfortable to everyone involved—based on a survey that you provide. For the freelance designer, such peers could include clients, vendors, and other freelancers. There are thousands of sites on the web that

provide guidance for conducting such an evaluation, but the key factor is asking questions that yield useful results (as opposed to simply "interesting" results) and then acting on what you discover.

For example, a pertinent question might be, "In which of these areas could I improve?" Offer multiple choice answers such as "Prompt response to phone calls or emails," "Listening skills" or "Adequate organization." Don't include things like price or areas of expertise if you have no intention of changing them.

Can a 360-degree evaluation be painful and scary? Certainly, but it allows the freelancer to act on and improve core competencies before there is any loss of business. It is an especially useful tool for people who work alone; in offices, employees are usually evaluated at least once per year by a supervisor. A freelancer could work for years in a complete vacuum.

If you do conduct a 360-degree evaluation, remember that you are learning others' perceptions of your professional self. For instance, if a client indicates that you would benefit from improvement in listening, even though you think you are a very good listener, remember that for the client, that perception is a reality. Look for ways to improve rather than be personally offended or simply ignore the feedback.

Continuing education

Read any book or take any course on being successful in business and the one thing they will all have in common is stressing the importance of being a lifelong learner. Continuing education can be as simple as following an online tutorial or as involved as taking a college degree. In between are seminars, conferences, workshops, books, magazines, and much more—even the right blogs or regular skill-sharing sessions between colleagues can be tremendously helpful. One freelancer interviewed for this book reported that, after she or a designer friend attended a conference or workshop, they would get together over dinner and share new skills or insights.

Ongoing educational opportunities are plentiful, but finding the time to take advantage of those opportunities is another matter. Time away from work (that is, generating income) can be hard to justify.

"To find the time for our education is very important," says Adrian Abdala. "To take a break from our work is a debit, but it must be seen as an investment and not as a loss."

Eleni Swengler, a freelancer from Baltimore, US, agrees. "As someone who earned a Master of Fine Arts degree and taught design at the college level for four years, I strongly believe that education does not end upon graduation. Our only job security nowadays is our knowledge. The more we know, the more valuable we are to our clients," she says.

Because time is always limited, though, careful choices must be made from the myriad educational opportunities.

"The key is to filter the things that you need to know, the things that are nice to know, and the things that you should know just in case, from all of the junk," advises Eduardo Peixoto, a freelancer based in Oregon, US.

Changing direction

Moments may arise when it is clear that something has to change. Maybe it's time for a completely new business strategy.

Eleni Swengler notes a period several years ago when most of her freelance jobs were turning into production work, with very little room for creativity. Then a large client took its design work in-house.

"That's when I knew I needed to develop a marketing strategy to find better work. I focused my efforts on a few segments where I have experience, such as education

❶ When asked to help write an education course for other artists, Savyra Meyer was intimidated. She has worked as a designer and illustrator, but had never done anything like this before. Ultimately, the project fulfilled a dream for the artist, enabling her to pass on what she had learned to others.

"If you are in design for material things, you are going the wrong way."
Christian Steagall-Condé, Freelance designer, Brazil

1 A designer can stretch his capabilities with new and very different projects. Freelance designer Ronn Lee was asked by The Gourmand Group to create a custom coffee gift set for corporations. The project required the "free play of creativity," says Lee, who came up with the product names, the colors, and the packaging.

and health care. It's easier to get a foot in the door with these industries because I have a proven track record and have numerous printed samples to show," she says.

South African freelance designer Savyra Meyer also experienced a crisis that turned into a blessing. Unwisely, she admits now, she had taken on four large clients, all in the same business sector. When that sector went dry for a year, taking away 80 percent of her income, she was forced to sell her house and use some of the profit to study animation and web design.

"It opened new vistas for me. I was totally rejuvenated," she says. "It was a disaster that occurred at precisely the right time for me."

Occasionally, the signs may even indicate that it's time to leave the freelancing life. The most common reasons for leaving freelancing that were cited by designers interviewed for this book were (in no particular order):

1. Inadequate income/benefits
2. Feeling isolated or wanting to be part of a larger team
3. Lack of personal satisfaction
4. Loss or lack of creativity
5. A desire to try something different.

"You know that it's time to move on when you no longer see the benefit in working independently; when you no longer enjoy providing your services to clients; when you are no longer profitable; or when you no longer feel that the quality of your work can compete in the market," adds freelancer Maneesha Lee Jones from Florida, US.

Any one or a combination of these factors is reason enough to consider becoming employed by someone else or trying out a new line of work. But don't look at the change as an end or a failure. Instead, consider it as an exciting opportunity to use your specialized skills in a new way that can help different people. And don't rule out freelance design forever. A number of designers interviewed for this book have enjoyed the freelance life at two or three different times in their lives.

1

Expanding your business

Responses to this issue usually fall into one of two distinct camps: freelancers either definitely want to expand their business or they absolutely do not. Deciding to have employees is an enormous step, one that will change the fundamental nature of your business and your role. You're no longer a freelancer but an employer. The security of another person or persons now depends on you. And if you're someone who enjoys your solitude, you will no longer work alone.

But how do you know whether you should expand your business? One factor is if business is so brisk that it is impossible to handle it all on your own. Perhaps you are frequently bringing in other freelancers, or maybe there is a certain type of work that must always be farmed out (programming or production, for example). Maybe you just need office help, even part time.

Another promising indicator is when long-term clients have indicated that they will be calling on you as long as they are able. You might also have been offered larger jobs that you were unable to handle as a small shop. Or, perhaps through awards or other recognition, your visibility has grown to the point where the time is simply right.

But to expand, there must be money.

"In order to be a master of your destiny or craft, you must first learn to be a good servant. For the freelance graphic designer, this means serving your client by listening actively to what they need and want; providing good collaboration; and providing design services that surpass what is expected while knowing when to change your design without compromising the integrity of the design, the project, the client, or the designer."

Nathalie Bertin, Visual Funk!, Ontario, Canada

"Your financial indicator will determine when to expand your business," explains Shahud R. Shami, a freelancer based in Islamabad, Pakistan. "To be a successful business, I will always need a copy person, an accountant, and so on. The moment you feel you can hire people, do it. It will nourish your business, and you will be able to utilize your skills more effectively."

When you reach this point, a once-a-year financial examination will not be adequate. Instead, chart your finances over an extended period. Compare recent numbers to figures from the previous year to gauge progress. Are you making money all of the time, or just in certain seasons? The income from your business must support employees year-round.

Hiring employees also brings with it a whole host of legal and tax issues. Speak with your accountant and lawyer before moving forward.

❶ Freelance designer Stacey Dyer had a double sense of progress in her career when a local United Way benefit asked her to donate something for a charity auction: she created a certificate good for five hours of design time. Her business, Triple Frog, had been recognized as a community entity, and it gave her the opportunity to stretch her talents. "At the time, I was longing for my fine-art education to come back and slap me, just to let me know I still had it. With this little piece, the design is an homage to *The Figure Five in Gold* by Charles Demuth," she says.

1

LIVE LONG AND PROSPER

Nathalie Bertin of Visual Funk! in Ontario, Canada, offers 10 recommendations for a long and happy life as a freelance creative:

1 Complete the workbook *The Artist's Way*, by Julia Cameron (Tarcher, 1992)

2 Take a business course.

3 Take an accounting course.

4 Take any course that suits you.

5 Get a financial advisor, a lawyer, and an accountant who have a thorough knowledge of the design industry and/or who have designers as clients.

6 Read books.

7 Go somewhere different once a week—a new city, restaurant, or museum, for instance.

8 Go for walks or go dancing.

9 Laugh a lot.

10 Plan for inevitable economic downturns as much as you do for making money.

Featured Designers

Adam Hansel, Deadvolt Designs
www.deadvoltage.com

Adam Hayes
www.mrahayes.co.uk

Adrian Abdala
www.adrianabdala.com.ar

Amy McAdams
www.amymcadams.com

Amy Stafford, Blixa 6
www.blixa6.com

Bill Pandos
billpandos@yahoo.com

Brooke Goans
www.originalspaperart.com

Camillia BenBassat, Avec
avec.us

Carly Franklin, CFX Creative
www.cfxcreative.com

Carolina Amaya
www.carolinaamaya.com

Cecilia Melli
ceciliamelli@yahoo.it

Charlotte Fritzberg, Blick Design
www.blickdesign.co.uk

Chris Robinson
www.crobbo.com

Cinthy Pilar Revilla Llanos
cinthy.revilla@gmail.com

Craig Hansen
chansen74@hotmail.com

Damang Chassianda Sarumpaet
damang.sarumpaet@gmail.com

Emily Alston
www.emilyforgot.co.uk

Eric Benoit
www.ebenoit.com

Ivancka Kroell
ivancka@hoochiemamma.co.za

James Christian
www.groundfresh.net

Janice Davis
www.janicedavisdesign.com

Javier Escalante
ja@ellaboratorio.com.mx

Jennifer Wambach
www.jenniferwambach.com

Jens Mebes, Spincycle
www.washspindry.com

Jill Anderson, Jill Lynn Design
www.jilllynndesign.com

Jose Nieto, Square Zero
www.squarezerostudio.com

Joseph Harries
www.josephharries.com

Karen Chase, 224 Design
www.224design.com

Karolina Pluska
piszdomnieteraz@gmail.com

Kelly Hansen, Scooter Creative
www.scootercreative.com

L. Steven Pashley, L S Pashley
   Interactive Design
lspashley.com

Lidia Varesco
www.lsvdesign.com

Lisa Sarkees, Studio L
www.studiolworks.com

Maciej Hajnrich, Valp
www.valpnow.com

Minaksi Jena
meeeshaa@gmail.com

Prashant Chauhan, Zero 9
www.zero9.in

Radim Malinic, Brand Nu
www.brandnu.co.uk

Savyra Meyer
www.savyra.com

Scott Jessop
scott_jessop@btinternet.com

Sebastián Litmanovich, TeaTime Studio
www.teatimestudio.com

Seth Meierotto, BarkinSpider Studio
www.barkinspider.com

Søren Severin
www.sorenseverin.dk

Stacey Dyer, Triple Frog
www.triplefrog.com

Sue Hoffman
www.suehoffmandesigns.com

Susanna Edwards
www.susannaedwards.com

Tracie Haner Valentino
www.traciedesigns.net

Yomar Augusto
www.yomaraugusto.com

Resources

Helpful organizations for freelancers

AIGA
www.aiga.org

Creative Freelance Conference
www.creativefreelancerblog.com

Freelance Camp
freelancecamp.org

Freelancers Union
www.freelancersunion.org

Graphic Artists Guild
www.gag.org

Creative staffing firms

24 Seven
24seveninc.com/index.php

Aquent
www.aquent.com

Artisan
www.artisancreative.com

Big Creative
www.bigcreative.com

Big Fish
www.gobigfish.com

Choice Creative
www.choicecreative.com

Creative Circle
www.creativecircle.com

The Creative Group
www.thecreativegroup.com

Filter
www.filtertalent.com

Paladin
www.paladinstaff.com

Publicis
www.publicis.com

Job boards for freelancers

AIGA
www.aigadesignjobs.org/public/jobs_browse.asp

Authentic Jobs
www.authenticjobs.com

Behance Network
www.behance.net

Coroflot
www.coroflot.com

Creative Hot List
www.creativehotlist.com

Design:related
designrelated.com/jobs

Elance
www.elance.com

Freelance Switch
freelanceswitch.com

Guru
www.guru.com

Jobs&Gigs
jobsandgigs.com

Krop
www.krop.com

Smashing
jobs.smashingmagazine.com/freelance

Time-tracking software for purchase

AcuInvoice (Online invoice and estimating software)
www.acuinvoice.com

Basecamp (Web-based project management service)
www.basecamphq.com

Bento (Personal organizational software)
www.filemaker.com/Bento

Clients & Profits
www.clientsandprofits.com

Copper (Project management software)
copperproject.com

Creative Manager Pro (Ad agency project management software)
www.creative-manager.com

DesignSoft/StopWatch
www.designsoft.com

Easy Time Tracking (Time management and customer billing software)
www.easytimetracking.net /index.asp

FourteenDayz (Online time-tracking software)
www.14dayz.com

FreshBooks (Online time tracking and invoicing software)
freshbooks.com

FunctionFox/TimeFox
www.functionfox.com

Harvest (Online time-tracking software)
getharvest.com

JobCapture (Project management software)
www.captureworks.com

LiveTimer
www.livetimer.com

PunchyTime (Online time-management software)
www.punchytime.com

@Task (Project and portfolio management software)
www.attask.com

Tempo (Online time-tracking software)
keeptempo.com

YaTimer (Time management software)
www.nbdtech.com/ yaTimer

Time-tracking freeware

Remember the Milk (Online task management software)
www.rememberthemilk.com

Ta-da Lists (Online to-do list service)
www.tadalist.com

Billing software

BlinkBid
blinkbid.com

Blinksale
www.blinksale.com

CurdBee
www.curdbee.com

Freshbooks
www.freshbooks.com

QuickBooks
search.quickbooks.com

SimplyBill
simplybill.com

Index

Acknowledgments

As always at the end of a design book project, I feel grateful and indebted to all of the wonderful designers who so generously agreed to share their insights and work. I had the opportunity to meet amazingly generous freelance designers from all over the world. It's very gratifying to learn that there are so many people (like me) who are benefiting from and growing in the freelance life, in places familiar and exotic. We all seem to share the same worries, the same drive, and the same love of having control over our own lives.

I'd like to offer special thanks to two successful freelance designers who reviewed all of the book's text:

• Rodney Davidson of DogStar Design (www.dogstardesign.com) has been creating graphic design for many years. He lives and works in Birmingham, Alabama.

• Charlotte Fritzberg (www.blickdesign. co.uk) set up her own studio, Blick, after leaving Pentagram in April 2008. She lives and works in London.

In addition, I'd like to thank Tegan Blackburn (Tegan Blackburn LLC, Simsbury, Conn., www.teganblackburn.com), who was kind enough to review Chapter 6. Tegan has counseled clients for two decades on a wide variety of art law, business law, intellectual property issues, and other commercial areas. (The material in Chapter 6 is not intended to be legal advice and is offered for general informational purposes only.)

The lovely staff at RotoVision is also due many thanks. Team RV has brought me several wonderful opportunities to learn and grow, and the staff could not be more patient and kind in their guidance.

Finally, I must thank my wonderful family—three great sons who (to my delight) are each actively involved with drawing and design, and husband Denny, who has no involvement whatsoever but who is forever patient with and encouraging of visually oriented people who would rather sketch on a checkbook than balance it.

Cathy Fishel-Lane